Understanding Ethics in Early Care and Education

Nancy Baptiste
New Mexico State University

Luis-Vincente Reyes
New Mexico State University

PEARSON

Merrill
Prentice Hall

Upper Saddle River, New Jersey
Columbus, Ohio

Library of Congress Cataloging-in-Publication Data

Baptiste, Nancy E.

Understanding ethics in early child care and education / Nancy E. Baptiste,
Luis-Vincente Reyes.

p. cm.

Includes bibliographical references

ISBN 0-13-112055-7 (pbk.)

1.Early childhood teachers—Training of—United States. 2. Early childhood
teachers—Professional Ethics—United States. 3. Early childhood education—
Moral and ethical aspects—United States. I. Reyes, Luis-Vicente. II. Title

LB1732.3B36 2005

372.11—dc22   2004040021

Vice President and Executive Publisher: Jeffery W. Johnston
Publisher: Kevin M. Davis
Development Editor: Julie Peters
Editorial Assistant: Amanda King
Production Editor: Sheryl Glicker Langner
Design Coordinator: Diane C. Lorenzo
Cover Design: Harold Leber
Cover Image: Corbis
Production Manager: Susan Hannnahs
Director of Marketing: Ann Castel Davis
Marketing Manager: Autumn Purdy
Marketing Coordinator: Tyra Poole

This book was set in Times Roman by Prentice Hall. It was printed and bound by R. R.
Donnelley & Sons Company. The cover was printed by Coral Graphic Services, Inc.

Pearson Prentice Hall™ is a trademark of Pearson Education, Inc.
Pearson® is a registered trademark of Pearson plc
Prentice Hall® is a registered trademark of Pearson Education, Inc.
Merrill® is a registered trademark of Pearson Education, Inc.

Pearson Education Ltd.   Pearson Education Australia Pty. Limited
Pearson Education Singapore Pte. Ltd.   Pearson Education North Asia LtLtd.
Pearson Education Canada, Ltd.   Pearson Educación de Mexico, S.A. de C.V.
Pearson Education–Japan   Pearson Education Malaysia Pte. Ltd.

10 9 8 7 6 5 4 3 2 1
ISBN: 0-13-112055-7

Acknowledgments

- Martha Flynn, Prentice Hall Associate Editor, remained patient and supportive of the revision/expansion process

- Lynn Hicks, Prentice Hall Publisher's Representative who urged us to consider this project

- Ann Davis, Prentice Hall Editor, who graciously provided encouragement, support, and feedback

- Students enrolled in early childhood courses who read the early drafts of the book

- Members of the faculty of the New Mexico State University "Publish Don't Perish" team who read and critiqued excerpts of the book

- "Publish Don't Perish" team leader, Laura Madson, who provided constructive feedback on two chapters

- Dr. Herman Garcia, head of the Department of Curriculum and Instruction, College of Education, New Mexico State University who continuously asked "How's it going?" and provided ongoing encouragement

- Colleagues who generated excitement and energy about the book

- Steve Jeffries, Technology Fellow, who provided technical and technological assistance

- Leah Welch, Early Childhood Graduate Assistant, who patiently read and edited the final drafts

- Atalia D'nae Coleman, for her four years of continuing inspiration

➤ Sandra Leopold, for her technical assistance in formatting the completed document

➤ Evangeline Ward, Lilian Katz, and Stephanie Feeney for recognizing and acknowledging the importance of ethics in the early care and education profession.

➤ Spirit Winds Coffee Shop for providing an environment conducive to our creative work.

Preface

Primary concerns in the field of early care and education are the needs for an enhanced dialogue with pre-service students and practitioners about ethics and for avenues to expand the awareness, understanding and application of the NAEYC (National Association for the Education of Young Children) Code of Ethical Conduct. The authors of this text, both professors in an early childhood program, have embraced these concerns because in their review of books, journals, and other resource materials for their courses, they have found that there is limited reference to the NAEYC Code of Ethical Conduct (hereafter referred to as NAEYC Code). It is only recently, through the impetus of two NAEYC publications, that early care and education courses have begun to address more comprehensively the study of the NAEYC Code. The authors, by writing *Understanding Ethics in Early Care and Education*, have created an additional resource for students, practitioners and families to enhance their understanding of ethics in early care and education and the NAEYC Code.

There are two overarching goals that serve as the framework for the writing of *Understanding Ethics in Early Care and Education*. The first goal addresses the authors' attempt to encourage the reader to both examine the beliefs that will guide his/her ethical behavior and expand his/her knowledge, skills and attitudes regarding ethical practice. To accomplish this, the authors focused the text on four Guiding Questions: 1) How has the profession addressed the issue of professional ethics? 2) What do you do when your personal and professional values conflict with the values of your profession? 3) What resource can an early care and education practitioner use for resolving ethical dilemmas? and 4)How do we extend our understanding of ethics in early care and education? Part I, addresses the first Guiding Question by examining the historical development of the NAEYC Code and reviewing its conceptual framework and content. The second Guiding Question is addressed in Part II by assisting the reader to explore his/her relationship with the NAEYC Code by examining his/her personal and professional self. Part III addresses the third Guiding Question by providing opportunities for practice in applying the NAEYC Code and a Review Process for analyzing and resolving ethical dilemmas. The last Part addresses the final guiding questions by supporting the reader's exploration of two issues and assisting the reader to think differently about ethics in early care and education.

The second overarching goal is to offer an interactive text based on adult learning principles that enable readers to engage in reflective practices to enhance their understanding of ethics in early care and education. The major learning strategy is dialogue or a continuous sharing of knowledge and experience as suggested by Carter and Curtis (1994) and Vella (1995). The assumptions that guide the authors' thinking about the readers' learning is that learning occurs through active engagement in reading, dialoguing and reflection (Vella, 2000). Each Part includes activities adapted by the authors from Carter and Curtis (1994) and Vella (1995) e.g., Guiding Questions, What I Know, What I Have Learned, and Celebrating Our Understanding activities. The authors hope that the activities provided throughout the text will encourage the reader to engage in deep self- reflection related to ethics in early care and education and specifically to the NAEYC Code.

We trust that you will find *Understanding Ethics in the Early Care and Education* enjoyable reading and a contribution to the expansion of your knowledge, skills, and attitudes in early care and education ethics. We hope that this expanded knowledge will serve you well in your daily ethical practice with young children and their families.

—Nancy Baptiste and Luis-Vicente Reyes

Discover the Companion Website Accompanying This Book

The Prentice Hall Companion Website: A Virtual Learning Environment

Technology is a constantly growing and changing aspect of our field that is creating a need for content and resources. To address this emerging need, Prentice Hall has developed an online learning environment for students and professors alike—Companion Websites—to support our textbooks.

In creating a Companion Website, our goal is to build on and enhance what the textbook already offers. For this reason, the content for each user-friendly website is organized by topic and provides the professor and student with a variety of meaningful resources. Common features of a Companion Website include:

For the Professor—

Every Companion Website integrates **Syllabus Manager™**, an online syllabus creation and management utility.

- **Syllabus Manager™** provides you, the instructor, with an easy, step-by-step process to create and revise syllabi, with direct links into Companion Website and other online content without having to learn HTML.

- Students may logon to your syllabus during any study session. All they need to know is the web address for the Companion Website and the password you've assigned to your syllabus.

- After you have created a syllabus using **Syllabus Manager™**, students may enter the syllabus for their course section from any point in the Companion Website.

- Clicking on a date, the student is shown the list of activities for the assignment. The activities for each assignment are linked directly to actual content, saving time for students.

- Adding assignments consists of clicking on the desired due date, then filling in the details of the assignment—name of the assignment, instructions, and whether or not it is a one-time or repeating assignment.

- In addition, links to other activities can be created easily. If the activity is online, a URL can be entered in the space provided, and it will be linked automatically in the final syllabus.

- Your completed syllabus is hosted on our servers, allowing convenient updates from any computer on the Internet. Changes you make to your syllabus are immediately available to your students at their next logon.

For the Student—

- **Introduction**—General information about the topic and how it will be covered in the website.
- **Web Links**—A variety of websites related to topic areas.
- **Timely Articles**—Links to online articles that enable you to become more aware of important issues in early childhood.
- **Learn by Doing**—Put concepts into action, participate in activities, examine strategies, and more.
- **Visit a School**—Visit a school's website to see concepts, theories, and strategies in action.
- **For Teachers/Practitioners**—Access information you will need to know as an educator, including information on materials, activities, and lessons.
- **Current Policies and Standards**—Find out the latest early childhood policies from the government and various organizations, and view state, federal, and curriculum standards.
- **Resources and Organizations**—Discover tools to help you plan your classroom or center and organizations to provide current information and standards for each topic.
- **Electronic Bluebook**—Paperless method of completing homework or essays assigned by a professor. Finished work can be sent to the professor via email.
- **Message Board**—Virtual bulletin board to post and respond to questions and comments from a national audience.

To take advantage of these and other resources, please visit the *Ethics in Early Care and Education* Companion Website at

www.prenhall.com/baptiste

CONTENTS

Part I

DEVELOPING AN AWARENESS OF THE
NAEYC CODE

Reviewing the Historical Development of the NAEYC Code.

"Walking Through" the Conceptual Framework, Content, and Context of the NAEYC Code.

DEVELOPING AN AWARENESS OF THE NAEYC CODE

In Part I, you will expand your knowledge of the NAEYC Code by reading about its historical development and framework. "Knowing" about the history, conceptual framework, content, and context of the NAEYC Code will help you enlarge your personal and professional construction about ethics in the early care and education profession. As you engage in the reading and activities in Part I, you will have an opportunity to identify and expand what you already know about the NAEYC Code. You will also synthesize what you have learned and understood and celebrate your effort. Learning about the history, conceptual framework, content, and context of the NAEYC Code will guide your understanding of early care and education professional ethics.

GUIDING QUESTION

The guiding question that frames Part I is:

- How has the early care and education profession addressed professional ethics?

To assist the reader in answering the guiding question for Part I, we will review the development of the NAEYC Code from its inception to its current status and examine the conceptual framework, content, and context of the NAEYC Code.

Reviewing the Historical Development of the NAEYC Code

**What I Know Activity:**

To begin naming what you already know about ethics in the early care and education profession, please respond to the following statements:

1. What I know about ethics in the early care and education profession is...

2. What I know about the framework, content, and context of the NAEYC Code is...

The field of early care and education, also known as early childhood education, has continuously faced the challenge of becoming a profession. One of the major challenges that the field has overcome has been the movement from an occupation to a profession. Historically, child care has been associated with "watching children"/"babysitting;" the idea was that anyone could do this work regardless of whether or not they liked children or had the required knowledge bases to work with children. As bodies of knowledge have emerged in the areas of child development, growth and learning, health safety and nutrition, developmentally appropriate practice, family and community collaboration, and assessment, so have the demands for the professional training of individuals. Concomitant with the expanded knowledge bases was the recognition that early childhood embraced both education and care and needed its own professional nomenclature to describe its programs, personnel, and services. A nomenclature would assist the profession in appearing like other professions.

Similar to other professions, the field of early care and education incorporated certain characteristics that have distinguished it as a profession. Vander Ven (1986), from her review of the sociological literature, listed the following elements of a profession which have been contextualized to the early care and education profession:

- "an established knowledge base," (e.g., in early child-hood, child development, health, safety and nutrition, etc.)
- "a controlled entry into the field," (e.g. Career Lattice)
- "a value system around service, including a code of ethics," (e.g., NAEYC Code)
- "the needs of clients are defined by the profession," (e.g., types of services)
- "autonomous practice," (e.g., exercising professional judgment)
- "a specialized education system embracing both the knowledge base and delivery skills," (Ade, 1982; Spisak, 1983; Davies-Jones, 1985, p. 14). (e.g., professional preparation programs from the Entry Level to the Doctorate)

Over the years, the profession has made great strides in their professionalization effort. The membership of the early care and education profession realized that because of its unique "client" population that it must create a non-traditional paradigm of professionalization. Bredekamp and Willer (1993) tell us "traditional routes to professionalism have tended to establish exclusionary, hierarchical systems of credentials resulting in increased costs and creating greater distance between professionals and clients without necessarily improving quality of service" (p. 83). The profession of early care and education has to be wary that it does not lose sight of its mission to provide the highest quality of services by its most educated professional members. Bredekamp and Willer (1993) state: "We already see this trend in child care in which increased qualification and status tend to come only with positions that move further away from direct contact with children" (p. 83). The profession wants to ensure that its members with its highest level of education are providing direct services to children and their families and are not distanced from their clients, that is, individuals with advanced degrees are working directly with children in classrooms and with their families rather than in administrative positions that require minimal contact with children.

The clients of the early childhood profession are defined as "adults and children for whom services are provided by adults." For example, the early care and education profession defines its clients as individuals for whom services are provided that include children and their

4

families, colleagues, and community. Children receive direct services such as care/education, physical, mental health, and nutrition, among others from adults. The services provided to families by adults may include child care, preschool or public school education, referral, and possibly social services, employment skill training, transportation, and ESL classes. Colleagues receive professional employment, professional development opportunities, and collegiality from adults. The community receives high quality care/education programs, services, and information for its members from adults. To address the complexity of these interactions, the profession moved toward the development of a code of ethical conduct, one of the elements from Vander Ven's list of characteristics of a profession. The profession of early care and education, based on its beliefs of the advantage of professionalizing, today offers its members a code of ethical conduct. This code is based on the foundation that, "professionals not only agree to operate according to a high standard of behavior, but they also agree to monitor the conduct of others. In a field such as ours, in which regulations are minimal and exempt many settings, the protection of children demands that all individuals working with children conform to the highest standards of ethical conduct" (Bredekamp & Willer, 1993, p. 84). In addition to protection for children, the code provides guidance for relationships with families.

The regular contact of families and their children's care/educators create increased opportunities for conflicts often due to different value systems. Conflicts include but are not limited to issues of parent's rights, children's rights, appropriate curriculum, guidance techniques, child abuse and neglect, and cultural and linguistic responsivity. It has been the ethical dilemmas, conflicts, and questions in the field that have led the profession to develop a code of ethical conduct. With the increase in the number and type of conflicts, practitioners needed guidelines to address the variety of situations they were encountering in their everyday practice.

The guidelines needed by the profession are framed in the concept of ethics. The concept of ethics addresses conflicts and has historical roots in all professions. Ethics has to do with human well being, and the issue of power. According to Nash (1996) as suggested by Angeles (1992), ethics also has to do with examination of "ought, should, duty, right, wrong, obligation and responsibility" (p. 2). Professions that have human beings as "clients" need to assist their members in making professional judgments and in protecting their "clients." In the early care and education profession, "big people" have power over "little people." The early care and education profession needs to provide safeguards for its multiple clients, children and families. Thus, ethics provides a format for professional value, ideals, and principles that practitioners can use to guide their professional behavior. Nash (1996) states "A code of ethics embodies the highest moral ideals of the profession" (p. 96). Without a code of ethics to guide professional behavior, the early care and education profession was at a loss.

To illustrate how the profession was at a loss without a code of ethics, Luis-Vicente, one of the authors, shares how he grappled with issues of what he thought were right for children and how parents sometimes disagreed. As a former program director, he remembers having lengthy discussions with parents regarding spanking as a way of disciplining young children. He did not support that type of discipline because he believed that there were better ways of helping children to learn to self-regulate. Without a code of ethics to support his position, that of not spanking children, his work with parents who believed that spanking was the best way to discipline was most challenging. Today, with a code of ethics as support, he would be more readily able to defend his position. The current NAEYC Code provides practitioners with Core Value, Primary Responsibilities, Ideals and Principles to guide their decision-making and practice. Practitioners need for guidance about everyday practice impacted the inception and development of the code more than thirty years ago.

The early care and education profession began its work on a code of ethics with the challenge by Evangeline Ward in the mid 1970s to develop a draft of a code of ethics. In 1976, the governing board of NAEYC, the professional organization, agreed to develop a Code of Ethical Conduct. Lilian Katz promoted dialogue about ethics suggesting that there were some unique elements for early childhood and that it was important for the profession to have a code. According to Katz and Ward (1989), the need for the code emanated from a range of ethical problems related to: 1) power and status of practitioners, 2) multiplicity of clients, 3) ambiguity of data base, and 4) role ambiguity. The clients included children, families, communities and colleagues who represented a wide range of needs to be served. Katz and Ward, said, "a Code of Ethical Conduct may help practitioners cope with the ambiguities with greater success" (p. 15). They also said that, "If we are further to establish ourselves as professionals, we must set high ethical and professional standards by creating conditions for the protection of children, their families and the profession" (p. 19). At the same time the profession issued a call for the development of a code of ethics, an individual state adopted a Code of Ethical Conduct Responsibilities. The Minnesota AEYC created a code of their own with thirty-four principles to make sure that all early care and education professionals in the state of Minnesota had appropriate guidance for their practice.

To represent the professions needs at the national level, NAEYC, in 1984, appointed a commission to draft a code based on the work of Katz and Ward. Stephanie Feeney was appointed Chairperson and spent five years studying and drafting the Code of Ethical Conduct. Stephanie Feeney's commission studied, reflected upon and dialogued in depth about the development of the Code by inviting participation from the membership of the profession in order to get an inclusive view of what a code of ethical conduct should look like.

The process began in 1985 with a survey distributed to the NAEYC membership, through the NAEYC journal, *Young Children*. The commission received six hundred responses to its survey. Three hundred and thirty-one of the responses described ethical dilemmas. Ninety-three per cent of the respondents said the professional organization should immediately focus on development of the code because of the seriousness of the dilemmas and "ethical pain" experienced by practitioners as described by Kipnis in Feeney and Freeman, (1999). The second step involved conducting ethics workshops throughout the country. The focus of the workshops was "What should the good early childhood educator do when?" The third step was to publish ethical dilemmas in *Young Children* and solicit responses from the membership. The fourth step was to actually draft a code that was presented at the annual NAEYC conference in November 1988. The actual code, entitled the NAEYC Code of Ethical Conduct, was approved by the NAEYC Board in 1989 and published in *Young Children* in November 1989. Feeney and Freeman (1999) described the code "as a living document, designed to be responsive to changes in the Associations membership, the moral climate of our society, and new challenges faced by the profession" (pp. 17–18). To assure that the document is dynamic, the code is reviewed and revised every five years.

In addition to the Code, the profession developed a Statement of Commitment (p. 28). The purpose of the commitment statement was to recognize that the only way the NAEYC Code can continue being a viable professional document was for each practitioner to adhere to the code in order to further the value of the early care and education profession. Additionally, the commitment statement seeks to urge each practitioner to make a commitment to honor the Code. The development of the NAEYC Code was inclusive of many of its members. The professional organization wanted to encourage its membership to continue to dialogue about the Code. The profession recognized the work done by Feeney and others involved in the development of the Code as a hallmark of the profession.

Currently NAEYC has made a commitment to heighten its members' awareness and understanding of the NAEYC Code. By offering a variety of workshops on ethics at both its yearly national and professional development conferences, the organization offers opportunities for its membership to dialogue about professional ethics. In addition, the organization makes available the NAEYC Code brochure in two languages, English and Spanish. From time to time, *Young Children,* the journal of NAEYC, publishes articles related to ethics and urges comments and feedback from the membership.

To date, the current NAEYC Code addresses the ethical challenges of early care and education practitioners. The NAEYC Code does not include guidance for early childhood higher education faculty and the ethical dilemmas they face as a result of a culturally and linguistically diverse student population. Members of the profession are currently discussing the next steps in ethics development and drafting materials that are inclusive of guidance for higher education faculty as they experience a variety of ethical dilemmas.

Now that we have learned about the historical development of the NAEYC Code, it is time to synthesize our learning by responding to reflective questions. While you are completing the "What I Have Learned" activity, we will begin preparation for a discussion in the next part about the document description, conceptual framework, content, and context of the NAEYC Code.

What I Have Learned

Reflective Questions

If you are in a classroom setting, "Think, Pair, and Share" (Wolfe, 2000). Think about your response to the question, find a partner, and share your responses. If you are not in a classroom setting, share your thoughts with a friend.

1. How would you describe the process of developing the NAEYC Code?
2. What was most exciting to you about the development of the NAEYC Code?
3. Why do you think it is important that the NAEYC membership participated in the development of a Code of Ethical Conduct?
4. What process would you develop for including the diverse members of the early care and education profession (practitioners, administrators, students, etc.) in the next revision of the NAEYC Code?

"Walking Through" the Conceptual Framework, Content, and Context of the NAEYC Code of Ethical Conduct

 **What I Know Activity:**

The NAEYC Code consists of core values, ideals and principles. Please read the following examples and respond to the questions.

Examples:

- ❑ Respecting the dignity, worth, and uniqueness of each individual (child, family member, and colleague).
  1. What name (core values, ideals, or principles) would you give to this example from the NAEYC Code?
  _____

- ❑ I.1.1 To be familiar with the knowledge base of early care and education and to keep current through continuing education and in-service training.
  2. What name (core values, ideals, or principles) would you give to this example from the NAEYC Code?
  _____

  P-1.1 Above all, **we shall not harm children**. We shall not participate in practices that are disrespectful, degrading, dangerous, exploitative, intimidating, emotionally damaging, or physically harmful to children. This principle has precedence over all others in this Code.

  _____

  3. What name (core values, ideals, or principles) would you give to this example from the NAEYC Code?

  _____

  4. How would you describe the differences between core values, ideals and principles?

In this section of Part I, we will discuss the conceptual framework and contents of the NAEYC Code. We encourage you, the reader, to thoroughly review and refer to the NAEYC Code document at the end of this chapter. First, let us remind ourselves of what a code of ethics is. Clyde and Rodd (1989) state: "A code of ethics, is a set of value judgments relating to the way in which the person or group should behave in order to uphold or abide by the professional value of that group" (p. 2). In the case of the NAEYC Code, the core values, primary responsibilities , ideals, and principles represent the "value judgments" of the members of the profession.

In order to learn about the Conceptual Framework of the NAEYC Code, we will start by examining the Preamble, which states the reason for the Code, what the Code includes, and the primary focus of the Code. We will then look at the core values, primary responsibilities , ideals, and principles of the NAEYC Code. These five aspects of the document comprise the conceptual framework and contents of the NAEYC Code. Finally, we will look at the Statement of Commitment. The entire Code represents "an official position statement of the National Association for the Education of Young Children."

The Preamble, the first part of the document, sets the tone for the NAEYC Code. The Preamble says that the Code is primarily for practitioners who work on a daily basis with children although there are some applicable sections for people who do not work directly with children such as program administrators and college professors. The Preamble also to reminds us that the Code applies to practitioners serving children birth through age eight in a variety of early care and education settings to include, but not be limited to, public/private funded preschools, child care centers, family child care homes, Head Start Programs, kindergartens, and primary classrooms up to third grade. Now that we know that the Preamble specifies for whom the Code applies, we can continue examining the NAEYC Code.

Next, let us look at the core value in the NAEYC Code. The purpose of the core value is to establish the professions idea of what value are worthwhile as they relate to professional behavior. The core values represent "those value judgments" to which early care and education professionals are committed. Those value stem from value that have developed consensually and historically in the field, and relate specifically to relationships with children and families. Core values are not material things; they are abstract ideas, such as appreciation and recognition. The six core values are: 1) the appreciation of childhood as a unique developmental stage; 2) basing our work on knowledge of child development; 3) appreciating and supporting the close ties between the child and family; 4) recognition that children are best understood in the context of family, culture, community, and society; 5) respect for the dignity, worth and uniqueness of each individual; and 6) helping children and families reach their full potential.

The core values provide a disposition for our thinking about how we need to behave on a daily basis and help us to understand the conceptual framework of the code. For example, one of the core values is recognizing that children are best understood and supported in the context of family, culture, community, and society. To demonstrate how that core values will guide the teacher, we will use curriculum planning as an example. When the teacher is developing curriculum for young children, he or she will involve families in the planning and implementation of the curriculum to ensure responsiveness to children's language, culture, and their home. What might happen in a classroom in the southwestern part of the country is that the curriculum may include a tortilla-making activity as one of many activities to demonstrate that although different ethnic groups make and eat different kinds of bread, all ethnic groups have some kind of "bread food." Parents, grandparents, or other family members might be invited to the classroom to share in the tortilla making activity and discuss its home and cultural relevance to the child's life. The curriculum activity is responsive to some of the children's culture in that tortillas are a food that a child may recognize because she or he might be served tortillas at home. The activity expands the cultural experience of other children who may not have experienced this type of "bread" and who do not have an understanding of the universality of "bread food." The teacher, through this activity, is supporting one of the profession's core values. Teachers daily engage in practices that support this and other core values.

The next section of the Code, the Conceptual Framework, further reminds us of the "clients" of the early care and education profession. The code says there are four groups of people to whom early care and education practitioners have responsibilities: 1) children, 2) families, 3) colleagues, and 4) community members. In our profession, because we deal with dependent children, we must always have "other adults" in mind. Children require adults (parents, other family members, early care and education practitioners, and individuals in the community) to meet their needs. As we look at the Conceptual Framework of the Code, we see that in each section there is a description of ethical responsibilities, related ideals, and a description of principles.

In the first section of the Conceptual Framework we will find the Codes primary responsibilities. As mentioned previously, early care and education practitioners have ethical responsibilities to four groups of people. The Code defines these responsibilities as professional relationships that practitioners have with the selected four groups. To illustrate these relationships we will look at Section III, Ethical responsibilities to colleagues. The introduction states, "The same ideals that apply to children are inherent as our responsibilities to adults" (NAEYC Ethical Code of Conduct, 1997) whether we are working with co-workers, employers, or employees. Our primary responsibility in this area is to create environments that support collegiality and professional development for adults. The Conceptual Framework section also describes the ideals and principles in the Code and explains that ideals and principles represent agreed upon value of the professional membership.

The Code provides a set of ideals in each section. Perhaps the best way to think about the "ideals" of the Code is in terms of "how we should behave." Practitioners can use the ideals as signposts of expected behavior that supports their professional responsibilities to children, families, colleagues, community, and society. What is important to know is that ideals represent those behaviors that the profession expects its practitioners to demonstrate. For example, Ideal I-1.1 states, "to become familiar with the knowledge base of early childhood care and education and to keep current through continuing education and in-service training." One way the practitioner can use this ideal to guide his/her behavior is by becoming aware of and participating in community training and state, regional, and national conferences. Practitioners may enhance their professional practice by attending professional training and contributing to the quality of professional services. Another way practitioners may enhance their professional knowledge is to regularly read professional journals such as *Young Children* and *Child Education International.* There are always multiple ways to actualize the ideals of the Code. The ideals in each section precede the principles of the Code.

Principles might best be thought about as "right thinking." Principles are compelling guides for an active conscience. We always need to stay alert and reflect on our practice as we relate to "others." For example, Principle P-1.1 is bolded and necessarily so: **Above all**

we shall not harm children. The Code says that this principle supersedes all other principles. This principle serves as a directive to practitioners to remind them of their responsibility to children. This principle tells practitioners in no uncertain terms that they may not harm children physically, emotionally, sexually or in any other way. The concept of harm always needs to be examined. Years ago, people readily spanked their children without awareness of the harm that can come to children. With advanced research we know that spanking is not appropriate as a guidance technique because it can cause both physical and psychological harm to children. From this example we can see how the context of guiding children has shifted, i.e., from accepting spanking as a guiding technique to eliminating spanking as a guiding technique. In this way the Code has been responsive to the context of professional knowledge of the profession. In the section that follows we will be discussing the context of the development of the NAEYC Code.

The development of the NAEYC Code is a hallmark in our profession. The Code emerged from the need for guidance in professional practice by a group of practitioners who were encountering ethical dilemmas in their daily professional practice with children, families, and colleagues. Prior to the development of the NAEYC Code, early care and education professionals were rendering services to children and families from an individual/community-based value system rather than a professionally based value system. For example, rather than receiving guidance for behavior and professionally determined value, individuals used guidance from their own or community- based value system, value that were not necessarily supported by a professional knowledge base and continuing research. As the profession moved toward professionalization, early childhood leaders lamented a lack of core values for the profession. The membership consensually created core value, a conceptual framework, and a statement of commitment to guide professional practice.

The NAEYC Code provides a reminder to practitioners to act responsibly and continue to revisit their commitment to the profession. For example, Nancy, one of the authors, says that every time she reads the NAEYC Code, she is reminded how important it is that everyone in the field be aware of the Code, know it, use it and critique it. She especially likes the Statement of Commitment at the end. The Statement says, "As an individual who works with young children, I commit myself to furthering the value of early childhood education as they are reflected in the NAEYC Code" and then lists commitment actions. Luis-Vicente, on the other hand, said that every time he reads the NAEYC Statement of Commitment, which he has many times during his career, he has been motivated to continue his professional development. For example, the Commitment Statement says, "Be open to new ideas and be willing to learn from the suggestions of others." He says that this statement causes him to continuously renew and refocus his practice.

The authors agree that ethics education workshops should be part of all professional training events to ensure that practitioners and prospective practitioners develop an understanding of the Code and that the profession continuously revisits the NAEYC Code. Built into the Code development process is the provision to revisit the Code every five years. As societal issues change, the profession has to ensure that the code is reflective of the professional context. It will soon be time to revise the NAEYC Code. The revision committee will need to hear the voices of the profession to ensure that the Code remains a dynamic document.

We invite you now to synthesize your learning by responding to the reflective questions provided in the "What I Have Learned" activity.

What I Have Learned

Reflective Questions

If you are in a classroom setting, "Think, Pair, and Share" (Wolfe, 2000). Think about your response to the question, find a partner, and share your responses. If you are not in a classroom setting, share your thoughts with a friend.

1. What have you learned about the conceptual framework and content of the NAEYC Code?
2. What is your response to learning about the NAEYC Code?
3. Why do you think it is important to thoroughly study the NAEYC Code?
4. What might be some changes you would make to the NAEYC Code?

Celebrating Our Understanding

In the first section in Part I, you learned about the historical development of the NAEYC Code. In the second section you examined the conceptual framework and content of the NAEYC Code. With this knowledge you are now able to answer the Guiding Question: "How has the early care and education profession addressed professional ethics?"

What is exciting to know is that you have expanded your construction of early care and education professionalism to include the language of ethics. It is important for practitioners to have this knowledge as a tool to guide professional decisions that need to be made on a daily basis.

Celebrate your effort in completing Part I and join us in Part II where you will begin to move from an awareness level to a deeper understanding of the NAEYC Code.

References and Resources

Bredekamp, S., & Copple, C. (Eds.). (1997). *Developmentally appropriate practice in early childhood programs* (Rev. ed.). Washington, DC: NAEYC.

Bredekamp, S. & Willer, B. (March, 1993). Professionalizing the field of early childhood education: pros and cons. *Young Children.*

Carter, M., & Curtis, D. (1994). *Teaching teachers: A harvest of theory and practice.* St. Paul, MN: Readleaf Press.

Clyde, M., & Rodd, J. (1989). Professional ethics: There's more to it than meets the eye. *Early Child Development and Care, 53,* 1–12.

Feeney, S, & Chun, R. (1985). Effective teachers of young children. *Young Children, 41*(1), 47–52.

Feeney, S., & Freeman, N. (1999). *Ethics and the early childhood educator: Using the NAEYC Code.* Washington, DC: NAEYC.

Feeney, S., Freeman, N. K., & Moravcik, E. (2000). *Teaching the NAEYC code of ethical conduct.* Activity Sourcebook. [Companion resource to ethics and the early childhood educator: Using the NAEYC Code]. Washington, DC: NAEYC.

Feeney, S., & Kipnis (1985). Professional ethics in early childhood education.*Young Children, 40*(3), 54–58.

Katz, L. G. (1995). *Talks with teachers of young children: a collection.* Norwood, NJ: Ablex.

Katz, L. G., & Ward, E. (1989). *Ethical behavior in early childhood education* (Expanded ed.). Washington, DC: NAEYC.

Katz, L. G., & Ward, E. (1978). *Ethical behavior in early childhood education.* Washington, DC: NAEYC.

Nash, R. (1996). *"Real world" ethics: Frameworks for educators and human service professionals.* New York: Teachers College Press.

Vander Ven K. (1986). And you have a ways to go: The current status and emerging issues in training and education for child care practice. In K. Vander Ven & E. Tittnich (Eds.), *Competent caregiver competent children: Training and education for child care practice* (pp. 13–34). New York: Haworth Press.

Vella, J. (1995). *Training through dialogue: Promoting effective learning with adults.* San Francisco, CA: Jossey-Bass Publishers.

Wolfe, B. (2000). Cooperative learning in the college classroom. Workshop at New Scripts Institute, North Carolina.

Adopted 1989
Amended 1997

Code of Ethical Conduct

Preamble

NAEYC recognizes that many daily decisions required of those who work with young children are of a moral and ethical nature. The NAEYC Code of Ethical Conduct offers guidelines for responsible behavior and sets forth a common basis for resolving the principal ethical dilemmas encountered in early childhood care and education. The primary focus is on daily practice with children and their families in programs for children from birth through 8 years of age, such as infant/toddler programs, preschools, child-care centers, family child care homes, kindergartens, and primary classrooms. Many of the provisions also apply to specialists who do not work directly with children, including program administrators, parent and vocational educators, college professors, and child care licensing specialists.

Core Value

Standards of ethical behavior in early childhood care and education are based on commitment to core value that are deeply rooted in the history of our field. We have committed ourselves to

- Appreciating childhood as a unique and valuable stage of the human life cycle
- Basing our work with children on knowledge of child development
- Appreciating and supporting the close ties between the child and family
- Recognizing that children are best understood and supported in the context of family, culture, community, and society
- Respecting the dignity, worth, and uniqueness of each individual (child, family member, and colleague)
- Helping children and adults achieve their full potential in the context of relationships that are based on trust, respect, and positive regard

Conceptual Framework

The Code sets forth a conception of our professional responsibilities in four sections, each addressing an arena of professional relationships: (1) children, (2) families, (3) colleagues, and (4) community and society. Each section includes an introduction to the primary responsibilities of the early childhood practitioner in that arena, a set of ideals pointing in the direction of exemplary professional practice, and a set of principles defining practices that are required, prohibited, and permitted.

The ideals reflect the aspirations of practitioners. **The principles** are intended to guide conduct and assist practitioners in resolving ethical dilemmas encountered in the field. There is not necessarily a corresponding principle for each ideal. Both ideals and principles are intended to direct practitioners to those questions which, when responsibly answered, will provide the basis for conscientious decision-making. While the Code provides specific direction and suggestions for addressing some ethical dilemmas, many others will require the practitioner to combine the guidance of the Code with sound professional judgment.

The ideals and principles in this Code present a shared conception of professional responsibility that affirms our commitment to the core value of our field. The Code publicly acknowledges the responsibilities that we in the field have assumed and in so doing supports ethical behavior in our work. Practitioners who face ethical dilemmas are urged to seek guidance in the applicable parts of this Code and in the spirit that informs the whole.

Ethical dilemmas always exist

Often, "the right answer"—the best ethical course of action to take—is not obvious. There may be no readily apparent, positive way to handle a situation. One important value may contradict another. When we are caught "on the horns of a dilemma," it is our professional responsibility to consult with all relevant parties in seeking the most ethical course of action to take.

Section I: Ethical responsibilities to children

Childhood is a unique and valuable stage in the life cycle. Our paramount responsibility is to provide safe, healthy, nurturing, and responsive settings for children. We are committed to support children's development, respect individual differences, help children learn to live and work cooperatively, and promote health, self-awareness, competence, self-worth, and resiliency.

Ideals

I-1.1. To be familiar with the knowledge base of early childhood care and education and to keep current through continuing education and in-service training.

I-1.2. To base program practices upon current knowledge in the field of child development and related disciplines and upon particular knowledge of each child.

I-1.3. To recognize and respect the uniqueness and the potential of each child.

I-1.4. To appreciate the special vulnerability of children.

I-1.5. To create and maintain safe and healthy settings that foster children's social, emotional, intellectual, and physical development and that respect their dignity and their contributions.

I-1.6. To support the right of each child to play and learn in inclusive early childhood programs to the fullest extent consistent with the best interests of all involved. As with adults who are disabled in the larger community, children with disabilities are ideally served in the same settings in which they would participate if they did not have a disability.

I-1.7. To ensure that children with disabilities have access to appropriate and convenient support services and to advocate for the resources necessary to provide the most appropriate settings for all children.

Principles

P-1.1. Above all, we shall not harm children. We shall not participate in practices that are disrespectful, degrading, dangerous, exploitative, intimidating, emotionally damaging, or physically harmful to children. This principle has precedence over all others in this Code.

P-1.2. We shall not participate in practices that discriminate against children by denying benefits, giving special advantages, or excluding them from programs or activities on the basis of their race, ethnicity, religion, sex, national origin, language, ability, or the status, behavior, or beliefs of their parents. (This principle does not apply to programs that have a lawful mandate to provide services to a particular population of children.)

P-1.3. We shall involve all of those with relevant knowledge (including staff and parents) in decisions concerning a child.

P-1.4. For every child we shall implement adaptations in teaching strategies, learning environment, and curricula, consult with the family, and seek recommendations from appropriate specialists to maximize the potential of the child to benefit from the program. If, after these efforts have been made to work with a child and family, the child does not appear to be benefiting from a program, or the child is seriously jeopardizing the ability of other children to benefit from the program, we shall communicate with the family and appropriate specialists to determine the child's current needs; identify the setting and services most suited to meeting these needs; and assist the family in placing the child in an appropriate setting.

P-1.5. We shall be familiar with the symptoms of child abuse, including physical, sexual, verbal, and emotional abuse, and neglect. We shall know and follow state laws and community procedures that protect children against abuse and neglect.

P-1.6. When we have reasonable cause to suspect child abuse or neglect, we shall report it to the appropriate community agency and follow up to ensure that appropriate action has been taken. When appropriate, parents or guardians will be informed that the referral has been made.

P-1.7. When another person tells us of a suspicion that a child is being abused or neglected, we shall assist that person in taking appropriate action to protect the child.

P-1.8. When a child protective agency fails to provide adequate protection for abused or neglected children, we acknowledge a collective ethical responsibility to work toward improvement of these services.

P-1.9. When we become aware of a practice or situation that endangers the health or safety of children, but has not been previously known to do so, we have an ethical responsibility to inform those who can remedy the situation and who can protect children from similar danger.

Section II: Ethical responsibilities to families

Families are of primary importance in children's development. (The term family may include others, besides parents, who are responsibly involved with the child.) Because the family and the early childhood practitioner have a common interest in the child's welfare, we acknowledge a primary responsibility to bring about collaboration between the home and school in ways that enhance the child's development.

Ideals

I-2.1. To develop relationships of mutual trust with families we serve.

I-2.2. To acknowledge and build upon strengths and competencies as we support families in their task of nurturing children.

I-2.3. To respect the dignity of each family and its culture, language, customs, and beliefs.

I-2.4. To respect families' childrearing value and their right to make decisions for their children.

I-2.5. To interpret each child's progress to parents within the framework of a developmental perspective and to help families understand and appreciate the value of developmentally appropriate early childhood practices.

I-2.6. To help family members improve their understanding of their children and to enhance their skills as parents.

I-2.7. To participate in building support networks for families by providing them with opportunities to interact with program staff, other families, community resources, and professional services.

Principles

P-2.1. We shall not deny family members access to their child's classroom or program setting.

P-2.2. We shall inform families of program philosophy, policies, and personnel qualifications, and explain why we teach as we do? which should be in accordance with our ethical responsibilities to children (see Section I).

P-2.3. We shall inform families of and when appropriate, involve them in policy decisions.

P-2.4. We shall involve families in significant decisions affecting their child.
P-2.5. We shall inform the family of accidents involving their child, of risks such as exposures to contagious disease that may result in infection, and of occurrences that might result in emotional stress.
P-2.6. To improve the quality of early childhood care and education, we shall cooperate with qualified child development researchers. Families shall be fully informed of any proposed research projects involving their children and shall have the opportunity to give or withhold consent without penalty. We shall not permit or participate in research that could in any way hinder the education, development, or well-being of children.
P-2.7. We shall not engage in or support exploitation of families. We shall not use our relationship with a family for private advantage or personal gain, or enter into relationships with family members that might impair our effectiveness in working with children.
P-2.8. We shall develop written policies for the protection of confidentiality and the disclosure of children's records. These policy documents shall be made available to all program personnel and families. Disclosure of children's records beyond family members, program personnel, and consultants having an obligation of confidentiality shall require familial consent (except in cases of abuse or neglect).
P-2.9. We shall maintain confidentiality and shall respect the family's right to privacy, refraining from disclosure of confidential information and intrusion into family life. However, when we have reason to believe that a child's welfare is at risk, it is permissible to share confidential information with agencies and individuals who may be able to intervene in the child's interest.
P-2.10. In cases where family members are in conflict, we shall work openly, sharing our observations of the child, to help all parties involved make informed decisions. We shall refrain from becoming an advocate for one party.
P-2.11. We shall be familiar with and appropriately use community resources and professional services that support families. After a referral has been made, we shall follow up to ensure that services have been appropriately provided.

Section III. Ethical responsibilities to colleagues

In a caring, cooperative work place, human dignity is respected, professional satisfaction is promoted, and positive relationships are modeled. Based upon our core value, our primary responsibility in this arena is to establish and maintain settings and relationships that support productive work and meet professional needs. The same ideals that apply to children are inherent in our responsibilities to adults.

A. Responsibilities to co-workers

Ideals

I-3A.1. To establish and maintain relationships of respect, trust, and cooperation with co-workers.
I-3A.2. To share resources and information with co-workers.
I-3A.3. To support co-workers in meeting their professional needs and in their professional development.
P-3A.4. To accord co-workers due recognition of professional achievement.

Principles

P-3A.1. When we have concern about the professional behavior of a co-worker, we shall first let that person know of our concern, in a way that shows respect for personal dignity and for the diversity to be found among staff members, and then attempt to resolve the matter collegially.
P-3A.2. We shall exercise care in expressing views regarding the personal attributes or professional conduct of co-workers. Statements should be based on firsthand knowledge and relevant to the interests of children and programs.

B. Responsibilities to employers

Ideals

I-3B.1. To assist the program in providing the highest quality of service.
I-3B.2. To do nothing that diminishes the reputation of the program in which we work unless it is violating laws and regulations designed to protect children or the provisions of this Code.

Principles

P-3B.1. When we do not agree with program policies, we shall first attempt to effect change through constructive action within the organization.
P-3B.2. We shall speak or act on behalf of an organization only when authorized. We shall take care to acknowledge when we are speaking for the organization and when we are expressing a personal judgment.
P-3B.3. We shall not violate laws or regulations designed to protect children and shall take appropriate action consistent with this Code when aware of such violations.

C. Responsibilities to employees

Ideals

I-3C.1. To promote policies and working conditions that foster mutual respect, competence, well-being, and positive self-esteem in staff members.

I-3C.2. To create a climate of trust and candor that will enable staff to speak and act in the best interests of children, families, and the field of early childhood care and education.

I-3C.3. To strive to secure equitable compensation (salary and benefits) for those who work with or on behalf of young children.

Principles

P-3C.1. In decisions concerning children and programs, we shall appropriately utilize the education, training, experience, and expertise of staff members.

P-3C.2. We shall provide staff members with safe and supportive working conditions that permit them to carry out their responsibilities , timely and nonthreatening evaluation procedures, written grievance procedures, constructive feedback, and opportunities for continuing professional development and advancement.

P-3C.3. We shall develop and maintain comprehensive written personnel policies that define program standards and, when applicable, that specify the extent to which employees are accountable for their conduct outside the work place. These policies shall be given to new staff members and shall be available for review by all staff members.

P-3C.4. Employees who do not meet program standards shall be informed of areas of concern and, when possible, assisted in improving their performance.

P-3C.5. Employees who are dismissed shall be informed of the reasons for their termination. When a dismissal is for cause, justification must be based on evidence of inadequate or inappropriate behavior that is accurately documented, current, and available for the employee to review.

P-3C.6. In making evaluations and recommendations, judgments shall be based on fact and relevant to the interests of children and programs.

P-3C.7. Hiring and promotion shall be based solely on a person's record of accomplishment and ability to carry out the responsibilities of the position.

P-3C.8. In hiring, promotion, and provision of training, we shall not participate in any form of discrimination based on race, ethnicity, religion, gender, national origin, culture, disability, age, or sexual preference. We shall be familiar with and observe laws and regulations that pertain to employment discrimination.

Section IV: Ethical responsibilities to community and society

Early childhood programs operate within a context of an immediate community made up of families and other institutions concerned with children's welfare. Our responsibilities to the community are to provide programs that meet its needs, to cooperate with agencies and professions that share responsibility for children, and to develop needed programs that are not currently available. Because the larger society has a measure of responsibility for the welfare and protection of children, and because of our specialized expertise in child development, we acknowledge an obligation to serve as a voice for children everywhere.

Ideals

I.4.1. To provide the community with high-quality (age and individually appropriate, and culturally and socially sensitive) education/care programs and services.

I-4.2. To promote cooperation among agencies and interdisciplinary collaboration among professions concerned with the welfare of young children, their families, and their teachers.

I-4.3. To work, through education, research, and advocacy, toward an environmentally safe world in which all children receive adequate health care, food, and shelter, are nurtured, and live free from violence.

I-4.4. To work, through education, research, and advocacy, toward a society in which all young children have access to high-quality education/care programs.

I-4.5. To promote knowledge and understanding of young children and their needs. To work toward greater social acknowledgment of children's rights and greater social acceptance of responsibility for their well-being.

I-4.6. To support policies and laws that promote the well-being of children and families, and to oppose those that impair their well-being. To participate in developing policies and laws that are needed, and to cooperate with other individuals and groups in these efforts.

I-4.7. To further the professional development of the field of early childhood care and education and to strengthen its commitment to realizing its core value as reflected in this Code.

Principles

P-4.1. We shall communicate openly and truthfully about the nature and extent of services that we provide.

P-4.2. We shall not accept or continue to work in positions for which we are personally unsuited or professionally unqualified. We shall not offer services that we do not have the competence, qualifications, or resources to provide.

P-4.3. We shall be objective and accurate in reporting the knowledge upon which we base our program practices.

P-4.4. We shall cooperate with other professionals who work with children and their families.

P-4.5. We shall not hire or recommend for employment any person whose competence, qualifications, or character makes him or her unsuited for the position.

P-4.6. We shall report the unethical or incompetent behavior of a colleague to a supervisor when informal resolution is not effective.

P-4.7. We shall be familiar with laws and regulations that serve to protect the children in our programs.

P-4.8. We shall not participate in practices which are in violation of laws and regulations that protect the children in our programs.

P-4.9. When we have evidence that an early childhood program is violating laws or regulations protecting children, we shall report it to persons responsible for the program. If compliance is not accomplished within a reasonable time, we will report the violation to appropriate authorities who can be expected to remedy the situation.

P-4.10. When we have evidence that an agency or a professional charged with providing services to children, families, or teachers is failing to meet its obligations, we acknowledge a collective ethical responsibility to report the problem to appropriate authorities or to the public.

P-4.11. When a program violates or requires its employees to violate this Code, it is permissible, after fair assessment of the evidence, to disclose the identity of that program.

Statement of commitment

As an individual who works with young children, I commit myself to furthering the value of early childhood education as they are reflected in the NAEYC Code of Ethical Conduct.
To the best of my ability I will

- Ensure that programs for young children are based on current knowledge of child development and early childhood education.
- Respect and support families in their task of nurturing children.
- Respect colleagues in early childhood education and support them in maintaining the NAEYC Code of Ethical Conduct.
- Serve as an advocate for children, their families, and their teachers in community and society.
- Maintain high standards of professional conduct.
- Recognize how personal value, opinions, and biases can affect professional judgment.
- Be open to new ideas and be willing to learn from the suggestions of others.
- Continue to learn, grow, and contribute as a professional.
- Honor the ideals and principles of the NAEYC Code of Ethical Conduct.

This document is an official position statement of the National Association for the Education of Young Children.

This statement may be purchased as a brochure, and the Statement of Commitment is available as a poster suitable for framing. See our catalog for ordering information.

©1998 National Association for the Education of Young Children
Contact us at pubaff@naeyc.org
Updated

Part II

MOVING FROM AN AWARENESS LEVEL TO A DEEPER UNDERSTANDING OF THE NAEYC CODE

Exploring the Concepts of Personal Self and Professional Self

Examining and Practicing the Tools of Dialogue and Reflection

MOVING FROM AN AWARENESS LEVEL TO DEEPER UNDERSTANDING OF THE NAEYC CODE

In Part II, you will explore the relationship of your personal self (value, beliefs, experiences) and professional self (value, beliefs, and experiences) to the core value of the early care and education profession as expressed in the NAEYC Code. As you engage in the reading and activities of Part II, you will identify what you already know about the concepts of personal and professional self. You will also have an opportunity to learn about two tools, dialogue and reflection. The tools of dialogue and reflection can assist you when your personal and professional value conflict with the core value of the NAEYC Code. Additionally, you will synthesize what you have learned in Part II and celebrate your deeper understanding of the NAEYC Code. By using dialogue and reflection to enhance your understanding of your personal and professional value and their relationship to the professions core value you will move to a deeper understanding of the NAEYC Code. This deeper under-standing of the NAEYC Code will assist you in using the Code in your everyday practice.

GUIDING QUESTION

The guiding question that frames Part II is:
- What do you do when your personal and professional value conflict with the value of your profession?

To assist the reader in answering the guiding question for Part II, we will learn about the relationship between the practitioners' personal and professional value and the core value of the NAEYC Code.

Practitioners will also learn to use the tools of dialogue and reflection to assist them when conflicts occur between their personal and professional value and the core value of the NAEYC Code.

Exploring the Concepts of Personal Self and Professional Self

 **What I Know Activity**

Please read the following scenario and respond to the questions:

> Clara, a 24-year-old preschool teacher assistant, observes Thomas and Jonathan fighting over the yellow dump truck. Each child is trying to pull the truck away from the other. Clara knows that an NAEYC Code value is "appreciating childhood as a unique and valuable stage of the human life cycle". That value supports the principle "We shall not harm children" (P-1.1). With that knowledge, Clara redirects Thomas to play with the green dump truck.
>
> Clara has two children of her own, ages three and five. After a long day of working with the children of other families, she observes her daughter and son fighting over a bag of Fish crackers. Without hesitation she grabs the bag of Fish crackers and immediately spanks both children for fighting.

1. Describe Clara's professional value as expressed in the scenarios.
2. Describe Clara's personal value as expressed in the scenarios.
3. Describe how Clara's personal and professional value conflict.
4. Recall a situation when your personal and professional value conflicted.

Early childhood practitioners benefit professionally from exploring the concept of the personal and professional self. This exploration provides the practitioner with the understanding that assists him/her in

30

provides the practitioner with the understanding that assists him/her in resolving conflicts between personal and professional self value and the NAEYC Code value. Often the exploration begins with the questions: "Who am I?" and "Why do I have the value and beliefs that I do?" These questions that relate to ones personal self are questions that require responses when we are studying ethics in the early care and education profession. By responding to these questions we better understand our relationship with the professional value as expressed in the NAEYC Code. We will begin by examining the concept of personal self.

The personal self is that part of each of us that holds our value and beliefs, helps explain who we are, and guides our behavior. Culture and language serve as great influences on the personal self. What we know is that within cultures there exist differences. We are led to believe that if you belong to a particular cultural group, there are certain stereotypical behaviors that you demonstrate because you are a member of that group. For example, it is assumed that if you are a Hispanic you are able to speak Spanish. That assumption is erroneous because in fact not all Hispanics are able to speak Spanish. What we can learn from this example is that although one belongs to a cultural group, one does not necessarily assume all behaviors of that group. It is important to know that the personal self may or may not internalize all value from their particular contexts. Social theorists and researchers are continuously entertaining this discussion. A man named Pierre Bourdieu has given much thought to the development of the personal self.

Bourdieu (1991), born in France, gives us the idea of *habitus* to understand the personal self. What he says is that through the process of living, people acquire value and certain ways of knowing and behaving. This is what he calls *habitus*. For example, have you ever asked yourself why some people believe that brushing their teeth before showering is better than brushing their teeth after showering? Bourdieu might have said that there were models for either of those choices in the individual's home.

We know that what we see and hear in our interactions in our families, neighborhoods, communities, social organizations, and in society provide models for behavior and influence our developing values, which become part of the *habitus*. Bourdieu has described the process of being influenced by and adapting to others beliefs, values and behaviors as *inculcation*. The majority of our values come through *inculcation* from our homes, neighborhoods, communities, and society.

31

Those value and beliefs that we internalize through *inculcation* then guide our behavior.

Let us use the example of Clara in the scenario of her home to illustrate the concept of inculcation. We can say that Clara's personal self includes models and value of guidance that support spanking of young children. Those models and value may have come from her home, her religion, or culture. She might also tell you that she believes in spanking and that she value spanking as an appropriate guidance tool because her parents used spanking as a guidance tool. She might tell you that she believes inappropriate behavior of children must be responded to immediately with physical intervention. That is a belief and value that she has internalized through the process of *inculcation*. Her home, religion, community and culture support this value. The personal self comes to be through the process of *inculcation* as we interact with others and things in our environment. This is a continuing lifetime process. For example, when Clara married, the home that she and her husband created brought together two worlds of value and beliefs, perhaps some similar, perhaps some different. As their relationship emerged, their personal selves adjusted to any differences in value and beliefs. Thus, the personal self engages in many adjustments throughout the lifespan as a result of the *inculcation* process.

As we were writing, some of our own models and value came to mind. Luis-Vicente, one of the authors, said that boys in his family played with toys and materials that were designed for male play; for example, boys played with trucks and tools. When asked why that was the case, he said, it was not O.K. by the value and beliefs of my home and community for boys to play with dolls and gender specific dress up clothes. I had been *inculcated* by my home and community value to see specific role definitions for male and female child play. Nancy, on the other hand, believes that children regardless of gender should play with all types of toys and materials. Both her sons and daughter had their own dolls and trucks. When asked how she had come to that decision, she responded, in my family although there was role differentiation between my mother and father, they did not impose limitations on the behavior of their two daughters. My sister and I were encouraged to engage in diverse activities both indoors and outdoors, (e.g., yard maintenance, snow shoveling, fishing, rather than gender specified activities). As I look back, I guess I was *inculcated* with value of gender equity. As we have seen in the above examples, the inculcation of family value influences personal value.

As we examine the *inculcation* process for our professional value, we realize that as adults many of our value are influenced and affected by our professional experience and career preparation. Let us now look at the development of the professional self. The professional self emerges similarly to the personal self. The field of early care and education has continuously been engaged in the process of professionalization, that is, becoming a recognized, valued profession in our society. We know that the NAEYC Codes core value come from a collective effort of early care and education professionals throughout the country. This group of early care and education professionals, through consensus building, has offered a set of value to guide professionalism. In this scenario, Clara did not spank the fighting children in her childcare setting because she has been inculcated with the value promoted by her profession, in this case P-1.1 **Above all we shall not harm children**. The NAEYC Code is presented to students enrolled in professional preparation programs or through in-service staff development. In the process of professional development, students are being *inculcated* with a specified set of professional value to guide their professional behavior. The enforcement of these value lies within the profession itself (e.g., a child-care center setting in which the program director inculcates the staff with the professional value as expressed in the NAEYC Code). The director then monitors staff to ensure that the code guides their behavior. As we can then see, the professional self is created similarly to the personal self through the *inculcation* process. In this professional inculcation process, it is the profession that creates and supports the value.

Let us now revisit the scenario of Clara in her interactions with children in the center setting. We know that Clara believes that in her home spanking is an effective guidance tool. Spanking makes sense to her based on personal value. On the other hand, she adheres very closely to her professional code of ethics in her employment setting as evidenced by her use of redirection rather than spanking the children fighting over the same toy. The authors think that Clara's diverse behavior in two different settings demonstrates a conflict of her personal and professional value as reflected by the professions core value. Clara's behavior suggests a fragmented personal and professional self. What supports Clara's fragmentation is that there are specific values that guide Clara's behavior (i.e., home value that guide personal behavior at home and the core value of the NAEYC Code that guide Clara's behavior in her work setting). This conflict exists because Clara has not dialogued and reflected on why she behaves differently in the two settings. The conflict is detrimental to Clara as an early childhood practitioner because she is not aware of the discrepancy between her personal and professional self. She doesn't know that she doesn't know. When you understand the discrepancy between the value of your personal self and your professional self, and the NAEYC Code value, then you can understand why you behave differently in each of the settings.

Join us now in a conversation about how practitioners can use the tools of dialogue and reflection to reconcile their conflicts between personal and professional self and the NAEYC Code. While we are preparing for the discussion, you can be reflecting on the following questions.

What I Have Learned

Reflective Questions

If you are in a classroom setting, "Think, Pair, and Share" (Wolfe, 2000). Think about your response to the question/statement, find a partner, and share your responses. If you are not in a classroom setting, share your thoughts with a friend.

1. Identify two personal and two professional value you have. Briefly describe where you think they came from.
2. What is your feeling about having personal and professional conflicts?
3. Compare the NAEYC Code core values with your own personal value. Note where there is agreement and conflict.
4. How would you reconcile a conflict between a personal and professional value?

Examining and Practicing the Tools of Dialogue and Reflection

What I Know Activity

The difference between a conversation and dialogue is. . .

The process of reflection involves. . .

In this section of Part II, the authors will assist you in examining the use of two tools, dialogue and reflection, in the resolution of value conflicts between the personal and professional self and the NAEYC Code value. You are invited to read an expanded discussion of dialogue and reflection. You will read an example of this type of conflict between personal and professional value and the value expressed by the NAEYC Code. Last, you will see how the tools of dialogue and reflection can help in reconciling value conflicts.

A leader in the discussion of dialogue is the 19th century Brazilian educator Paulo Freire. Freire (1997), citing the work of the Austrian philosopher Martin Buber, tells us that for dialogue to happen the two individuals engaged in dialogue transform their "I"s to "Thou"s and thus, "meet in cooperation in order to transform the world" (p. 148). What this means is that when two individuals meet to dialogue, they meet not in a relationship in which one individual holds power over another, but in a relationship in which there is power shared between the engaged individuals. What individuals do when they engage in dialogue is that they critically analyze a reality-based problem. We will further elaborate on this using a scenario.

To further their professional development, two teachers, Melissa and Kathy, attended a workshop on literacy. As they reflected on what they learned at the workshop and what they had previously learned, they agreed it was not appropriate to formally teach three-year- olds to read despite what the materials the workshop presenters shared. They entered into a dialogue with their colleagues to further clarify their understandings and value. For both of them formally teaching preschool children to read was a reality-based problem. This concern was real to them in their everyday practice. As they entered into dialogue regarding the teaching of reading, the conversation might start with one thinking that she knows more than the other. Freire tells us that this is not dialogue. He says that according to Buber that one individual does not have power over the other. As the dialogue between Melissa and Kathy continues, they realize that one doesn't know more than the other and that each is making valuable, thoughtful, and insightful contribution to the dialogue. What has happened through the course of the dialogue is that each individual has come to understand that each has worthwhile contributions to the dialogue. Freire points to this stage of the dialogue as the point in which each individuals "I" becomes "thou." the power is now shared between them. This shared power between the individual and the realization that both have worthwhile contributions is known as cooperation.

It is this cooperation that leads to transformation or change in thinking about teaching reading to young children. The cooperative aspect of dialogue moves the individuals into action. Melissa and Kathy both decided, based on the cooperative aspect of dialogue, that by entering into dialogue with their colleagues at the center, they would be able to determine the appropriate action.

To further illustrate the use of dialogue, we will present the following scenario, you will read about a conflict between the personal and professional self and an NAEYC code values in which Stephanie, age 16, and Juan, age 18, are parents of Emma Joy, age two months.

Emma Joy is enrolled in the high school child-care center while Stephanie and Juan attend classes. Stephanie proudly tells Maria, the caregiver/teacher with sixteen years of experience and a Masters Degree in early care and education that every weekend regardless of the weather, she and Juan take Emma Joy to the high school football game. Maria thinks that Emma Joy is too young to sit in the cold in a large crowd at a football game. After all, when she was raising her children, she did not take them out until they were older and her Mom did not take her out as an infant. The first step Maria is taking to begin the dialogue process is to consult with her colleague, Dee, about her concerns. Dee asked Maria questions about the situation and reminded her about the NAEYC Code value that states a commitment to "appreciating and supporting the close ties between the child and family." Dee suggested that Maria talk about her concerns with Stephanie and Juan. After Maria takes Dees suggestion to talk to Stephanie and Juan, she learned that Emma Joy was dressed appropriately. Maria reflected on her own attitude and her discussion with Dee. Knowing that Emma Joy was dressed appropriately, was spending enjoyable time with both parents, and could continue to be nursed by her mom, Maria realized that there were some benefits to Emma Joy in this family outing. The next time that Stephanie told Maria that she and Juan were taking Emma Joy to the game, Maria said, "What a great idea. I am so glad that you are spending family time together."

What we are seeing in this scenario are conflicts in value between Maria's personal and professional self and the NAEYC Code. Maria's personal self informs her that infants should not be taken to football games. Her value is supported by her home value, that is, my mother never would have taken us as infants to football games and I did not take my own children as infants to football games. Maria's professional self is also in conflict with the NAEYC Code core value in that her professional training in health and safety issues related to infant care-giving supports her professional self-idea that infants should not be out in the cold in football games. Both Maria's personal and professional values are in conflict with the NAEYC Code value that supports close ties between the child and family. What helped Maria resolve the conflicts between her personal and professional value and those of the NAEYC Code value was dialogue and reflection with her colleague, Dee.

At this point in our discussion, we will discuss the two tools, dialogue and reflection, that can help to reconcile conflicts between the personal and professional self and the value of the NAEYC Code. We will use the example of Maria to provide greater clarity in the discussion of dialogue and reflection. Dialogue occurs when two individuals come together and have a conversation about their differing value for the purpose of understanding from where those values came. The reconciliation of Maria's personal and professional value that conflicted with the NAEYC core value began when she entered into dialogue with her colleague, Dee. Prior to Maria thinking that taking Emma Joy to the football game was a great idea, Maria held the personal value that an infant should not be taken to football games. Her personal value was supported by her upbringing and her assumption that she was a more mature mother than Stephanie. After all, she was twenty-six when she had her first baby and thought she was mature enough to know that infants should not be in the environment of a football game. Maria's professional values were also in conflict given that she has had formal training in health and safety issues related to infant caregiving. She had been reminded by her training that caregivers should inform parents of preventive health measures that support the well-being of the child. She believed that she should tell Stephanie and Juan that taking an infant out in the cold is not beneficial to the infant.

In addition to the tool of dialogue, reflection is a useful tool for resolving conflicts. Reflection occurs when an individual pauses during the dialogue to examine how his/her assumptions and value affect both thinking and behavior. The dialogue and reflection processes support the necessary thinking to change behavior. We can see from the example of Maria and Dee how the tools of dialogue and reflection can be helpful when personal and professional value conflict with the NAEYC Code value.

To further explain the use of dialogue and reflection to resolve conflicts, let us go back to our scenario. As you remember, Maria was concerned about Stephanie and Juan taking their young baby to a football game. Maria entered into a dialogue with her colleague, Dee. She shared with Dee her concerns about the inappropriateness of

Emma Joy attending the football games because of the cold weather and being in a crowd of people. She also mentioned to Dee that she has been an infant teacher for the past sixteen years, has been a parent, and has had formal training in infant/toddler care. Dee then asked Maria to think even more deeply about her value and beliefs and asked Maria about how her mother would have responded to this situation. Maria says that her mom never would have taken her to a football game as an infant and would have told her never to take her child to a football game at such a young age.

To help Maria gain more clarity in understanding her conflict, Dee shared with Maria that she had taken her infants to football games well dressed and there had been no ill effects. In fact, the outing had strengthened their family's relationship. Dee's information supported Maria in thinking more deeply about the value that were driving her concern. Dee also invited Maria to think about the NAEYC Code. She reminded her that one of the values of the Code is appreciating and supporting the close ties between child and family. Maria then told Dee that she really believes in appreciating and supporting the close ties between the child and family.

Thus, we see the power of dialogue between Maria and her colleague Dee. They had a rich conversation but also took a deeper look at the issues and challenged assumptions or "common sense" notions. Dialogue enables people to closely examine their value, assumptions and behaviors. Dialogue enables people to become aware of how their value impact their behaviors and how those value may conflict with other value, in this case, the NAEYC Code value.

In reviewing their conversation, we can see how Maria, with Dee's help, begins to reflect. Brookfield (1995), suggests that "talking to colleagues about problems we have in common and gaining their perspectives on these increases our chances of stumbling across an interpretation that fits what is happening in a particular situation" (p. 36). What Maria learns is that her conflict is between her personal and professional value and the value of the NAEYC Code. Dee's invitation to Maria to think about her value, both personal and professional, challenged Maria to reflect on the conflict. The reflection process enabled Maria to gain insight into why she wanted to tell Stephanie and Juan to refrain from taking their baby to the game. What she learned was that her way of thinking wasn't the only way of thinking about this issue. Her dialogue with Dee enabled her to have the courage to say to Stephanie and Juan, "What a great idea! I am so glad that you are spending family time together", because she examined through dialogue and reflection her personal and professional value and the NAEYC Code value. Maria's reflection of the experiences, assumptions, attitudes, and values supporting her previous thinking moved her to a new way of thinking and a new behavior that reconciled her conflict. According to Brookfield (1995), without the habit of reflection,

We run the continual risk of making poor decisions and bad judgments. We take action on the basis of assumptions that are unexamined. We fall into habits of justifying what we do by reference to unchecked "common sense" and of thinking that the unconfirmed evidence of our own eyes is always accurate and valid. (pp. 3–4)

We have explored Maria's conflict between her personal and professional value and the value of the NAEYC Code. Maria had a choice to maintain her current position, that is, suggest to the young parents that they keep their infant at home, or move to another position, which might be affirming the parent's decision and describing the benefit. Maria learned that utilizing the tools of dialogue and reflection gave her necessary information and insight to reconcile the conflicting value. As an early care and education practitioner, it is important to use the tools of dialogue and reflection for reconciling conflict that emerged between the personal and professional self-value and the value expressed in the NAEYC Code. The cooperative relationship that dialogue establishes moves early care and education practitioners into a space in which changes can occur.

What I Have Learned

Reflective Questions

If you are in a classroom setting, "Think, Pair, and Share" (Wolfe, 2000). Think about your response to the question/statement, find a partner, and share your responses. If you are not in a classroom setting, share your thoughts with a friend.

Dialogue occurs when individuals come together to have a conversation about an issue or topic. According to Vella (1995), "Dialogue assumes two human beings as subjects of their own learning, sharing research data, experience, and questions to transform both their own learning and the very knowledge they are examining"(p. 162). Dialogue differs from conversation in that dialogue requires that individuals not only engage in the conversation but also think about what has influenced their world view, that is, how home, community, education, experience, and culture, have influenced their thinking, values, and behavior. During dialogue the participating individuals equitably share power. Dialogue includes action as a result of your learning. For example, Rosemarie and Julia were concerned about the observation strategies they were using to learn about each child in their classroom. They engaged in dialogue about the best way to observe young children. They talked about the importance of observation, how and where they learned observation skills, their challenges in observing young children, and their use of information obtained from their dialogue about observations. This dialogue results in action by Rosemarie or Julia or by both of them. As the result of this dialogue, both Rosemarie and Julia decided to read books and attend workshops about observing young children.

1. Now that you know that dialogue involves conversation, shared power, reflection, and action, describe a time when you engaged in a dialogue about an issue related to early care and education.

Reflection occurs when an individual examines his/her own assumptions, experiences, values, and attitudes in relationship to a behavior, thought, or practice (Brookfield, 1995, pp. xii–xiii). In this reflective process, self-assessment moves one to take action. For example, after holding an infant in her arms for 15 minutes, Suzanne reflected on this experience. What she learned was that the infant she held gave her many cues (e.g. discomfort, grimacing, wiggling, crying, etc.), which told her that she needed to reexamine her behavior. She changed the position of the infant, and noted that the infant was now smiling, cooing, and showing less tension in his body.

2. Describe a time when you engaged in reflection on a care giving/teaching practice. Discuss how you changed your behavior.

Celebrating Our Understanding

In the first section of Part II, you analyzed the relationship between the personal and professional self and the core value of the NAEYC Code. In the final section of this Part, you examined the tools of dialogue and reflection. You engaged in reading about how the tools of dialogue and reflection facilitated by a colleague can assist the practitioner in resolving conflicts between personal and professional self and core value of the profession. What is exciting is knowing that as a practitioner you have tools available to you to use when value conflicts occur. These tools can help you to feel confident in the workplace. As a practitioner you need to feel confident in your professional judgment to ensure quality services for young children and their families.

Now celebrate your learning in Part II and join us in Part III where you will use a five-stage review process to analyze and resolve ethical dilemmas.

Resources and References

Bourdieu, P., & Passeron, J. (1991). *Language and symbolic power.* Cambridge, MA: Harvard University Press.

Brookfield, S.D. (1995). *Becoming a critically reflective teacher.* San Francisco, CA: Jossey-Bass Publishers.

Freire, P. (1997). *Pedagogy of the oppressed.* New York: The Continuum Publishing Company

Vella, J. (1995). *Training through dialogue. Promoting effective learning with adults.* San Francisco: Jossey Bass Publishers.

Part III

**EXPANDING OUR UNDERSTANDING OF THE
USE OF THE NAEYC CODE**

Exploring a Five-Stage Review Process for Resolving Ethical
Dilemmas

Using Scenarios to Practice the Five-Stage Review
Process for Resolving Ethical Dilemmas

EXPANDING OUR UNDERSTANDING OF THE USE OF THE NAEYC CODE

In the previous parts, you have learned about the NAEYC Code and about the use of the tools of dialogue and reflection in an effort to move from an awareness level to a deeper understanding of the use of the NAEYC Code. In this part, you will further expand your understanding of the use of the NAEYC Code by learning about a five-stage review process (referred to as the review process) for resolving ethical dilemmas. The review process consists of five-stages that can assist you in resolving ethical dilemmas and situations you confront in your challenging work with children and families.

As we know, and Herb-Brophy, Kostelnik, and Stein (2001) remind us, "ethical issues usually are ambiguous with no clear course of action readily apparent" (p. 82). As Nash (1996) suggests, ethical dilemmas are complex in nature and require consideration of several factors, including "the act, the intention, the circumstances, the principles, the beliefs, the outcomes, the virtues, the narrative, the community, and the political structures" (p. 20). Because of the complexity of ethical issues and the dilemmas that early care and education practitioners confront, the authors created a review process for resolving ethical dilemmas. A review process provides practitioners with guidelines to be used as part of their understanding, analysis and resolution of the ambiguities of ethical issues and/or dilemmas.

As you engage in the reading and activities in this part, you will have an opportunity to identify what you already know about resolving ethical dilemmas. You will learn about the review process for resolving ethical dilemmas and you will use scenarios to practice using the review process to resolve ethical dilemmas. Practice will assist you to develop the skills that you need in meeting the challenges of the ethical issues and dilemmas that you will encounter in your professional work. At the end of this part, you will also synthesize what you have learned in each section of the part and celebrate your understanding of the review process for analyzing and resolving ethical dilemmas. Knowledge of the NAEYC Code and review process for resolving ethical dilemmas will assist you in your professional journey as you encounter complex ethical dilemmas.

❑ What resource can an early care and education practitioner use for resolving ethical dilemma?

To assist the reader in answering the guiding question, we will learn about one resource. This resource is a Review Process created by the authors to resolve ethical dilemmas.

Exploring a Five-Stage Review Process for Resolving Ethical Dilemmas

Ethical dilemmas are ambiguous situations that invite different interpretations. Different interpretations arise from values, beliefs, and experiences that individuals bring to a situation. For example, have you ever seen or heard something and couldn't make sense of it? Perhaps what was missing for you was that you did not have a context (experience and understanding) for trying to understand that phenomena. The other thing that could have happened is that you used a way of seeing things that did not fit what you were seeing. Your perceptions impacted your understanding of that phenomena and how you acted on it. Imagine now, that you and your colleague are in a child care center and are having a conflict about the "rightness" or wrongness" of an interaction between a family and another teacher. You see the interaction from your world-view based on your models (value, beliefs, and experiences) that help you make sense of what you are seeing. However, your colleague sees the interaction from her world-view based on her models (value, beliefs, and experiences) that help her make sense of what she is seeing, and that model is quite different from yours. What is happening is that you and your colleague see alternative "right" ways of handling the situation. How will you resolve the value conflict? One way is for both of you to agree to use a review process to look at the situation. To explore the concept of the review process as a mechanism to assist us in resolving ethical dilemmas, you will have an opportunity to use scenarios to practice using the review process.

What I Know Activity

Please respond to the following question:
In the past, when you have encountered a professional value conflict, what resources have you used to resolve the value conflict?

_____

_____

To understand whether we are truly experiencing an ethical dilemma, we must know the difference between an ethical responsibility and an ethical dilemma. Let's begin learning about the differences so that we will know when to apply the proposed review process. The NAEYC Code identifies ethical responsibilities or standards of behavior agreed upon by the early care and education profession for each group of individuals with whom a teacher works: children, families, colleagues, the community, and society. An ethical responsibility guides the behavior of practitioners. For example, an ethical responsibility to children is: **We shall not participate in practices that discriminate against children by denying benefits, giving special advantage, or excluding them from activities on the basis of race, ethnicity, religion, sex, national origin, language, ability or the status behavior or beliefs of their parents** (NAEYC Code). From this NAEYC Code statement of ethical responsibility, we can see expectations for practitioner behavior supported by the professional knowledge base. Ethical responsibilities provide guidance to the practitioner but do not give specific solutions to conflicts. For instance, if Tomas hits Andrew over the head with a block, you will not find in the NAEYC Code either the words or actions you might use to handle this situation. What you will find are the general guiding principles that can support your decision-making. The ethical responsibility in the NAEYC Code that supports decision-making in this case is **"Our paramount responsibility is to provide safe, healthy, nurturing, and responsive settings for children"** (Section I). In this statement, one finds guidance rather than suggestions for specific actions or words

Sometimes we encounter a complex issue that has a moral component and possible costs and benefits to individuals. Such complex issues are called ethical dilemmas. Feeney and Freeman (1999) define an ethical dilemma as "a situation an individual encounters in the workplace for which there is more than one possible solution, each carrying a strong moral justification" (p. 24). Also, according to Feeney and Freeman (1999), "A dilemma requires a person to choose between two alternatives each of which has some benefits but also some costs" (p. 24). An ethical dilemma exists when core value from the NAEYC Code are in conflict. The core values represent the agreed-upon morality of the profession that provides the practitioner with an idea of professional right and wrong.

To further explain the definition of ethical dilemma, we will provide a scenario.

The mother of a three-year-old has asked you, the teacher, not to give her daughter a snack in the afternoon because it interferes with dinner. The mom believes that she has to give her daughter an early dinner so that she can get to her evening work shift on time. You have observed that the child is hungry at snack time. The dilemma: Should you meet the child's hunger needs by giving the child a snack or honor the mothers request to not give the snack to increase the possibility that the child will be able to eat an early dinner?

What we can see from this scenario is: 1) you have choices of solutions, 2) each solution includes costs and benefits, and 3) you are sensing a conflict in NAEYC core value. Your choices include: giving the child a snack at the regular snack time and increasing the chance the child will not eat dinner and that mom will be angry, not giving the child a snack at snack time and increasing the possibility that the child will be fussy and unable to participate in planned activities, or negotiating with the mom to give the child a snack earlier in the afternoon in an effort to satisfy the child's hunger needs and the moms need to feed her child an early dinner. The teacher believes that not feeding the child when hungry is wrong; however, she also believes that not respecting the requests of parents is wrong. In this situation there are costs and benefits for the mom, the child, and the teacher in each possible response. Ethical dilemmas stem from conflicts with the core value of the NAEYC Code. In this scenario, the core value that are being challenged are: "**Basing our work with children on knowledge of child development**" and "**Helping children and adults achieve their full potential in the context of relationships that are based on trust, respect and positive regard**" (Core Value, NAEYC Code). When a teacher asks herself or himself if the conflict has to do with right and wrong and the answer is "yes," then that teacher can conclude that there is an ethical dilemma. It is an ethical dilemma because there are two different ways of resolving this issue and each possible resolution has benefits and costs. For example, if the teacher feeds the child, the mother will be unhappy because her request was not honored, her schedule will be interfered with, and, as a result, she may consider moving her child to another program. If, on the other hand, the teacher honors the request of the mom, the child might be fussy and tired and unable to fully participate in planned activities in the program because her hunger needs are not met. Finding a resolution to ethical dilemmas requires practitioners to understand that one core value is being challenged by another core value and that there are alternative responses that have elements of morality and costs and benefits tied to them.

To further expand your ability to differentiate between ethical responsibility and ethical dilemmas, please read the following scenarios and identify each one as an ethical responsibility (ER) or an ethical dilemma (ED).

_____ 1. Mrs. Huerta, Lucas mother, has asked that you celebrate Lucas birthday with his friends in class. She brings to class a carrot cake, milk, and party favors for each child.

_____2. Jacob has been in time-out for 15 minutes because he did not stay in line when he was going to the cafeteria with his class. You question your teacher assistant as to why Jacob has been in time-out for such a long period. Your teacher assistant tells you that the reason that Jacob has been in extended time-out is that he obviously had not learned that it was not O.K. to get out of line. The teacher assistant believes that Jacob will come to understand that his behavior has to change as a result of extended time-out. She adamantly tells you that the goal is self-regulation.

1. Explain why you identified #1 as either an ethical responsibility or an ethical dilemma.

2. Explain why you identified #2 as either an ethical responsibility or an ethical dilemma

Hopefully, you identified #2 as an ethical dilemma for the teacher. There are many ways of addressing ethical dilemmas. The authors have created a five-stage review process as one way for resolving ethical dilemmas. The five-stage review process walks the practitioner through a systematic approach toward examining an ethical dilemma. The five-stage review process serves as a guideline similar to a road map that in turn will move the practitioner in the right direction toward the resolution of an ethical dilemma. For example, let's imagine that we are taking a car trip from Santa Fe, New Mexico to Washington D.C. Although we have a general idea about the location and distance between Washington, D.C. and Santa Fe, (i.e., about 2,000 miles), what we don't know is the exact route to get there. The logical solution to our problem would be to get a road map and figure out which highway to take to get to Washington, D.C. from Santa Fe. The five-stage review process serves as a road map to help the practitioner get from understanding the dilemma to taking action. Practitioners can resolve ethical dilemmas by using the review process and the NAEYC Code. The combination of the review process and the NAEYC Code provides clarification of the dilemma, which then positions the practitioner to exercise professional judgment that leads to action. Now that we have a conceptual model for resolving ethical dilemmas, let's examine closely the five-stages of the review process (see Figure 1).

Five-Stage Review Process for Resolving Ethical Dilemmas

⬇

Stage 1:
Apply to the situation a consistent definition of ethical dilemma

↿

Stage 2:
Use knowledge of the NAEYC Code of Ethical Conduct to guide personal and professional self-reflection and dialogue and reflections with a friend

↿

Stage 3:
Exercise and act on an ethical judgment

↿

Stage 4:
Reflect on the ethical judgment and explore opportunities for professional change

↿

Stage 5:
Facilitate professional change

Figure 1. A Five-Stage Review Process for Resolving Ethical Dilemmas

Stage 1

1. **Apply to the situation a consistent definition of ethical dilemma**

Figure 2. Stage 1 in the Five-Stage Review Process

The practitioner, in the first stage of the review process, uses a consistent definition to determine whether a situation constitutes an ethical issue. Everyday in practice you encounter challenging situations that have an ethical component. According to Nash (1996), an ethical issue involves questions of morality, right or wrong, and responsibility. Ethical issues address human well- being or what is in the best interests of those individuals with whom we work. The situation may be related to your work with children, families, colleagues, community, and society. Once a practitioner decides whether the issue has ethical considerations, he or she must next decide whether the situation involves an ethical responsibility or an ethical dilemma.

By using a consistent definition of ethical dilemma, practitioners know whether a situation is an ethical responsibility or an ethical dilemma. If the situation is determined to be an ethical responsibility, the practitioner exercises professional judgment as prescribed by the ethical responsibilities stated in the NAEYC Code. For example, an ethical responsibility (I-1.5) states, "**To create and maintain safe and healthy settings** . . . (NAEYC Code). Part of your role in maintaining a safe and healthy setting is to check the playground for safety or health hazards. If the situation is not deemed an ethical dilemma, the practitioner exercises his/her ethical responsibility. If the situation is deemed an ethical dilemma, the practitioner proceeds to **Stage 2** of the Review Process.

---

2. Use knowledge of the NAEYC Code of Ethics to guide personal and professional self-reflection, and dialogue and reflection with a colleague

---

Figure 3. Stage 2 in the Review Process

Essential to the resolution of an ethical dilemma is the use of the NAEYC Code. The second stage of the review process is to use knowledge of the NAEYC Code to guide dialogue and reflection with a colleague. Early care and education practitioners must have knowledge of the NAEYC Code as a framework to guide the analysis and resolution of ethical dilemmas. A practitioner can access the NAEYC Code in a variety of places including but not limited to: Chapter I of this book; Feeney and Freeman's book, *Ethics and the Early Childhood Educator; using the NAEYC Code,* the NAEYC website, *www. naeyc.org*; the NAEYC Code of Ethical Conduct brochure; local early care and education training and technical assistance; and/or child care resource and referral programs. The practitioner then uses his/her knowledge of the code to reflect and dialogue, as discussed in Part II. Reflection and dialogue are important tools to guide the practitioner into clarity of thought about right and wrong as agreed upon by the profession.

To illustrate the second stage of the review process, we would like to revisit the second scenario in Section 1 of this part.

The assistant teacher notices that Jacob is not staying in line when going to the cafeteria with his class. Without discussing Jacob's behavior with him, she puts him in time-out for 15 minutes. The classroom teacher believes that this is not an appropriate manner in which to address Jacob's behavior. The teacher then consults the NAEYC Code and specifies the conflicting core values: **"Basing our work with children on knowledge of child development"** and **"respecting the dignity, worth, and uniqueness of each individual child"** (NAEYC Code).

The teacher assistant must have believed that children of that age are able to stand in line. The teacher, on the other hand knows that not staying in line might be a developmentally appropriate response for a child of that age. The teacher believes that placing a child in "time-out" without an explanation of why he was placed there, neither respects the dignity, worth, and uniqueness of that child or promotes learning about his behavior.

The teacher then engages in personal and professional self-reflection. She reviews her personal value as well as her interpretation of professional value and standards of the profession. The teacher seeks out a colleague who could be the center director, a member of her professional organization, or other professional colleague. The teacher enters into a dialogue with her colleague, the classroom teacher in the next room. Brophy-Herb, Kostelnik, and Stein (2000) tell us that according to Nash (1996), "Providing opportunities for practitioners to talk about the basis of their actions may help novices understand and appreciate differences in judgment even when they do not agree with positions different from their own" (p. 82).

The teacher explains to her colleague her reference to the NAEYC Code and selection of the core value that she believes relate to the dilemma. The costs for the child include loss of self-esteem coming from his lack of understanding of why he had to sit in "time-out" and loss of learning to regulate his own behavior. Potential cost for the assistant teacher was loss of self-esteem and respect if negatively confronted by the teacher and her confusion about appropriate guidance. For the teacher, there was the potential for a change in the relationship with her assistant teacher because of differing viewpoints and value about supporting children's independent thinking. Her colleague asks her to delineate the costs and benefits of her possible responses. Her colleague then reflects to the teacher what she has heard in order to assist the teacher in gaining further knowledge about the situation. The colleague encourages the teacher to engage in personal and professional reflection and its relationship to the core value in conflict.

Some questions the colleague might ask the teacher during the dialogue to help the teacher clarify her thoughts and feelings include:

- What are you going to do?
- How do you feel about what you are going to do?
- Why is it important that you address this situation?
- What are you going to do next? (Spencer, 1989)

The teacher responded by saying that what she did was: 1) look at the NAEYC Code; 2) use her professional knowledge base; and 3) review her personal and professional value related to this situation. She stated that she was worried about her relationship with the teacher assistant and worried about the learning that was taking place for Jacob. She was also concerned that she was not adequately mentoring the teacher assistant. For her, the importance in addressing this dilemma was that it has implications for the child, for the teacher, and for the teacher assistant, as well as for professional change, i.e., in-service training. She stated that the action she will take is to invite the teacher assistant to join her in a comfortable environment to talk about her choice of guidance strategies.

Of course, the ideal is to reflect and dialogue with a colleague. However, we know in reality, oftentimes an ethical dilemma requires an immediate resolution. In this event, the practitioner would use the four questions indicated to reflect on the dilemma and then act on her decision. After the resolution of the dilemma, the practitioner might then seek out a colleague to further reflect on the resolution before moving on to Stage 3.

Stage 3

---

3. Exercise ethical judgment and act on a decision

Figure 4. Stage 3 in the Review Process

We have seen in the second stage of the review process how the practitioner engages in dialogue and personal and professional reflection to gain information about a situation. This information positions the practitioner to move to Stage 3 of the review process. The third stage of the review process invites the practitioner to exercise and act on ethical judgment.

Ethical judgment refers to the reflection of the practitioner on the information collected through the Stage 2 process. Once the ethical judgment is made, the practitioner acts on that knowledge. It is the practitioner's courage for resolving ethical dilemmas that transforms knowledge to action. This movement from knowledge to action also encompasses the acts of caring and creative thinking. I

In the case described above, the teacher knew that she had to take an action based on the information she had collected. She thought about how she was going to approach the teacher assistant regarding her guidance technique with Jacob. Her actual conferencing with the teacher assistant is the demonstration of her movement from knowledge to action through courage, caring, and creative thinking. In this scenario, she acts on her decision by entering into dialogue with the teacher assistant. She asks the teacher assistant why she chose "time-out" as a response to Jacob's behavior without discussing the situation with him. The teacher invites the teacher assistant to explore her position from both a personal and professional perspective. The teacher asks questions that help the teacher assistant to reflect on her actions. The teacher then proceeds to share with the teacher assistant that she has a dilemma because she is in disagreement with the teacher assistant's choice of action with Jacob and because she sees a conflict between two NAEYC Code core values. The teacher and teacher assistant discuss their differing opinions and the NAEYC Code core values and work toward reaching agreement. To accomplish this, the teacher enters into dialogue with the teacher assistant to facilitate an agreement.

Engagement in Stage 3 of the review process produced several outcomes. Through dialogue, the teacher assistant became aware of the personal and professional value that influenced her decision to put Jacob in "time--out" for 15 minutes. She realized that her guidance technique was based on her personal belief that children should be seen and not heard. The dialogue provided clarity so that she could rethink her guidance technique. She was able to assess the costs and benefits for the child and decided that it was worth a try to embrace another guidance method. The teacher assistant realized that without talking to Jacob about his behavior and placing him away from his peers for such an extended period of time, she was putting him at risk for lowered self-esteem and no behavioral change.

The teacher's suggestion that the teacher assistant engage the child in problem solving seemed to provide more benefits to the child by helping him to understand his choice of behavior. In fact, according to Reynolds (1996), using the problem solving method enhances a child's self esteem as he or she masters social and problem solving skills. In this situation the teacher exercised professional judgment by inviting the teacher assistant to dialogue with her. Once a practitioner exercises professional judgment and acts on a decision, she moves into the fourth stage of the review process.

---
4. Reflect on the ethical judgment and explore opportunities for professional change

---

Figure 5. Stage 4 in the Review Process

The fourth stage of the review process is the practitioners reflection on the exercised of ethical judgment and exploration of opportunities for professional change. Professional change refers to action that the practitioner will take to revise or modify an existing policy or practice. The ethical dilemma is the catalyst for identifying the policies or practices that enabled the occurrence of the ethical dilemma. In this stage the practitioner again conducts a self-talk that includes the questions:

- What did I do?
- How did I feel about it?
- Why was it important that I did what I did?
- What policy or practice that supported the ethical dilemma needs to be changed? (Spencer, 1989)

The practitioner's reflection in this stage has two purposes: 1) to reconcile and act on personal thoughts, feelings, or concerns related to the ethical dilemma, and 2) to provide information to move to the last stage of the review process.

In the aforementioned scenario, we saw how the teacher and teacher assistant through dialogue and reflection were able to reconcile the conflict between the NAEYC core values. The reconciliation can lead to follow-up activities, specific to the ethical dilemma. For example, the teacher might want to act on her personal reflection by touching base with the teacher assistant to ensure that there is no misunderstanding. The intent of this action is to safeguard the practitioner's personal and professional relationship. Another follow-up activity is for the teacher to determine through observation and discussion if the teacher assistant is continuing with the agreed-upon resolution strategy. The teacher can also evaluate the appropriateness and effectiveness of the resolution of the dilemma. For example, if talking to the teacher assistant does not produce changed behavior, then the teacher will need to seek an alternative strategy. Another key purpose of this reflection is to provide the practitioner with information needed to move into the final stage of the review process, that of creating professional change. It may be that the ethical dilemma red-flagged the need for the teacher to review the larger system.

Stage 5

5. Facilitate professional change

Figure 6. Stage 5 of the Review Process

In the final stage of the review process, the practitioner looks at the bigger context in which the ethical dilemma occurred. In the previous scenario, the bigger context of the ethical dilemma is professional development. The ethical dilemma described led the teacher to clearly understand that there is a need to review the in-service training component for teacher assistants. It seems that her teacher assistant lacked a current knowledge of the use of appropriate guidance techniques. The director might review in a systematic way the training needs of the staff. The format decided upon might include a system of follow up and feedback. For example, after a two-hour workshop on guidance, a staff member would practice using the new information, be observed using the new information, and then conference with the observer. In this scenario we saw how the review process assisted in the resolution of an ethical dilemma.

The final stage of the review process involves both reflection and action. The ethical dilemma may point to a center policy and/or practice that require review. The practitioner, through reflection and dialogue, has gained sufficient information to review and, if necessary, effect change in the organization.

The review process for the resolution of ethical dilemmas may address not only the ethical dilemma but also may pinpoint areas for improvement related to personnel, program procedures, curriculum, or other aspects of an early care and education program. The review process takes the practitioner on a journey that assists the practitioner to identify and resolve the dilemma, and move toward professional change. Practitioners using the review process can gain valuable information to promote quality and effectiveness in early care and education programs.

What I Have Learned

Reflective Questions

If you are in a classroom setting, "Think, Pair, and Share" (Wolfe, 2000). Think about your responses to the questions/statement. Find a partner and share your responses. If you are not in a classroom setting, share your thoughts with a friend.

1. What did you learn about the review process?
2. Why is each stage of the review process important?
3. What stage in the review process do you think will be most difficult for you and why?
4. Why is it important to use the five-stage review process for solving ethical dilemmas to facilitate professional change?

Using Scenarios to Practice a Five-Stage Review Process for Resolving Ethical Dilemmas

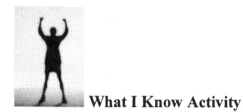 **What I Know Activity**

1. List the five stages of the review process.
2. Differentiate between an ethical responsibility and an ethical dilemma.
3. Describe the use of the tools of dialogue and reflection in the review process.

In this section, you will read a scenario and walk through the review process with the authors. The scenario will represent a complex ethical issue that an early care and education practitioner might encounter in his/her work. The authors will apply the five stages of the review process to this scenario through a dialogue. We will need to remind ourselves that there are not always easy answers for resolving ethical dilemmas and that the review process may cause discomfort. Ethical dilemmas require resolution through the use of courage, caring, and creative thinking.

You are an employee in a child care center. Your director announces at a staff meeting that beginning in a month, the center will be offering child care services on a 24-hour-per-day, 7-days-a-week schedule. She also announced that there would be three shifts to cover the 24-hour periods. Shift #1 is from 6:00 A.M. to 2:00 P.M. Shift #2 is from 2:00 P.M. to 10:00 P.M. Shift #3 is from 10:00 P.M. to 6:00 A.M. Currently there are nine children, two infants, four toddlers, and three preschoolers, who will need 48 hour, round the clock care because of their moms shifts at the hospital. They will be dropped off at 6:00 A.M. on Monday and picked up at 6:00 P.M. on Tuesday. You have been asked by the director to work shift #3 from 10:00 P.M. Monday to 6:00 A.M. Tuesday and shift #2 from 2:00 P.M. Tuesday until 10:00 P.M. on Tuesday.

The authors have selected this scenario which highlights the "marked changes in the nature, schedule and amount of work engaged in by parents of young children" (*Neurons to Neighborhoods,* 2000, p. 2) to demonstrate the use of the review process to resolve the ethical dilemma. The first stage of the review process asks us to apply a consistent definition to determine whether the situation is an ethical responsibility or an ethical dilemma. Feeney and Freeman's (1999) definition of ethical dilemma includes the following components: 1) more than one possible solution; 2) a choice between two alternatives, each of which has some benefits and some costs; and 3) a conflict between two NAEYC Code core value. In this scenario, the core values in conflict are: a) "**Basing our work with children on knowledge of child development**" and b) "**Recognizing that children are best understood and supported in the context of family, culture, community, and society**" (NAEYC Code).

These core values are in conflict for the practitioner because she believes that there is nothing in the knowledge base of child development that supports round the clock, out-of-home center care for young children. She also read the current research which states, "The consequences of the changing context of parental employment for young children are likely to hinge on how it affects the parenting they receive and the quality of the caregiving they experiences when they are not with their parents" (*Neurons to Neighborhoods* 2000, p. 9*)*. The practitioner, at the same time, also realizes that children are best understood and supported in the context of family. In these families, parents are required to work round-the-clock shifts in order to provide for their family. Centers providing family-friendly child-care services understand that extending their service hours is the best way of responding to and supporting family child-care needs.

The practitioner sees that there are two alternatives available to her. She can remain as an employee and work the shifts requested by her director despite the fact that she believes that it is wrong for children to be out of their homes in center care round the clock. Or she can resign and find employment in a child-care program that provides traditional out-of-home child care because she believes that round the clock, out-of-home child care does not support the developmental needs of children. The practitioner's identification of the conflicting core value, the recognition that she has alternative choices, and her understanding that the choices have costs and benefits satisfy the requirements of the first stage of the Review Process.

Having satisfied the first stage of the review process, the authors will engage in an abbreviated personal and professional self-reflection and dialogue and reflect with each other as colleagues to demonstrate the use of the second stage of the review process. Nancy will be the practitioner who has the dilemma. Luis-Vicente will be her colleague who is also employed as a teacher in the same center.

That evening, Nancy consulted her copy of the NAEYC Code to clarify the core value that seemed to be in conflict. She entered the second stage of the review process: **Use knowledge of the NAEYC Code of Ethics to guide personal and professional self-reflection and dialogue and reflection with a colleague** (NAEYC Code). Personally, she believed that children should not be in group center care for more than eight hours per day. Her experience is that she stayed home with her children while they were growing up because she valued family time together. Professionally, she could not think of one workshop or professional reading that supported seven-day-a-week, twenty-four-hour center-based care. She also believed that because there are no professional preparation materials or training available to practitioners to guide them in this extended-hour care-giving practice, it should not be available. The following morning, after tossing and turning for several hours during the night, she decided to enter into a dialogue with her colleague, Luis-Vicente (Stage 2):

Use knowledge of the NAEYC Code of Ethics to guide personal and professional self-reflection and dialogue and reflection with a colleague. Over coffee with Luis-Vicente, she explained that she doesn't know if she can continue working in the center because she believes that she has an ethical dilemma regarding the new family-friendly work schedule. She told Luis-Vicente that she has consulted the NAEYC Code and has reflected personally and pro-fessionally on the conflicting value. Luis-Vicente asked her to clarify her personal and professional reflections, that is, why the values are so conflicting for her.

L: "What did you find out about your personal value that contribute to the conflict?"

N: "As a mother of three, I would never leave my children in extended care. I don't think that children should be away from their families. It is just not right."

L: "Do you think that all families think like this or can survive without additional child care services? Have you ever considered that some families think that this is just fine?"

N: "You are probably right. I hadn't thought that some families might think that this is just fine for children I have been too caught up personally to think out of the box."

L: "What did you find out through your reflection about your professional self?"

N: "I just do not believe that based on our current knowledge of child development, children should be away from their families in center care, especially when I believe that teachers are not professionally prepared to provide extended care."

L: "Child care is an evolving practice and sometimes we find ourselves in situations that challenge our current knowledge base. It seems that at this juncture the overriding need is to meet family needs and provide care according to their schedules. Meeting family needs on schedules that are different from traditional schedules is a signpost of our changing society."

N: "Although I heard what you said, I am still troubled with the concept of providing extended care. I worry about the detriments to children, staff, and family. I feel as if I need to resign and find another center with traditional hours, but I don't want to leave the director in a pinch and I am worried as to how long it will take to find other employment. My children need food on the table."

Luis-Vicente proceeded to engage Nancy in further reflection by asking her four reflective questions.

L: "What are you going to do?"

N: "I just don't know. I feel so conflicted. I want to stand for my value but I am beginning to understand that as an early care and education practitioner, I need to expand my thinking. I don't want to leave the children at the child-care center; I like my director and the environment of the center. I need my salary to take care of my own family.

Luis-Vicente repeated the question: "What are you going to do?"

N: "I think I am going to try this new schedule. My children are older now and maybe I can adjust to a different time frame and still provide quality care. I will tell the director about my conflict."

L: "It seems to me that your have gathered the sufficient information for you to make a decision even though it is a hard one."

L: "How do you feel about what you are going to do?"

N: "I feel ambivalent and angry that I have to make this kind of choice. What are we doing to children and families?"

L: "Why was it important?"

N: "Because it really helped me to clarify the personal and professional conflicts that I had. I feel like I now have the courage, caring, and creative thinking to resolve this situation."

Then Luis-Vicente asked the last of the four questions, "What are you going to do next?"

N: "Despite how I feel about it, I am going to meet with my director and share my feelings. I will tell her that I will work the requested shifts but I will search for information about child-care centers that offer family-friendly schedules. I would also like the director to provide in-service training on "non-traditional child-care services."

From the responses to the four reflective questions that Luis-Vicente just asked, practitioners, in this case Nancy, can move into the third stage of the review process: **Exercise ethical judgment and act on a decision.**

We can see that Nancy, with the help of her colleague Luis-Vicente, has resolved the ethical dilemma and is ready to exercise ethical judgment and act on her decision, the third stage of the review process. Exercising ethical judgment requires the practitioner to further reflect on the information collected from the personal and professional reflection and the dialogue. Nancy again thinks about her personal and professional self and makes the decision to remain in her place of employment and enter into dialogue with her director. She acts on her decision by thinking about how she is going to address her director with her concerns. She then proceeds to ask her director if she would have coffee with her to discuss her concerns about the new center schedule. By asking to conference with the director, Nancy demonstrated her courage, caring, and creative thinking, which is the movement from knowledge to action.

After having conferenced with the director, Nancy moves into the fourth stage of the review process: **Reflect on the ethical judgment and explore opportunities for professional change**. That evening Nancy reflected on her conferencing with her director. Nancy's reflection identified opportunities for professional change in her center. She and the director have concluded that the issue of lack of professional preparation of staff for extended-hour center- based care continues to resurface. Nancy's courage, caring, and creative thinking had challenged her to make an appointment with her director to discuss this opportunity for professional change. The actual conferencing with her director about this change is the fifth stage of the review process: **Facilitate professional change.**

The outcome of the conference between the teacher and director was a commitment on the part of the director to establish a relationship with the local university to explore and examine the implications of extended care for children and families. The director, too, believed that extended center- based care is a real challenge to the program and agreed to provide in-service training prior to the beginning of the new shifts.

What the authors have demonstrated through the use of a scenario is the application of the five-stage review process for resolving ethical dilemmas. The review process for resolving ethical dilemmas takes a practitioner on a journey that is strategically designed to move the practitioner from the identification of the dilemma through the resolution of the dilemma. The process uses dialogue and reflection as tools to create the momentum necessary for professional change.

What I Have Learned

Reflective Questions

If you are in a classroom setting, "Think, "Pair, and Share" (Wolfe, 2000). Think about your response to the question, find a partner, and share your response. If you are not in a classroom setting, share your thoughts with a friend.

1. Review the scenario presented in the beginning of section 2 of this chapter (Nancy's ethical dilemma).
2. What feelings emerged for you as a result of Nancy's dilemma?
3. Using the scenario, role-play with your partner or friend Stage 2 of the review process. (Use knowledge of the NAEYC Code of Ethics to guide personal and professional self-reflection and dialogue and reflection with a colleague). Debrief your role-play by comparing and contrasting your dialogue with that of the authors.
4. Think back to ethical dilemmas you have experienced in the past and describe how the five-stage review process might have helped you resolve the dilemma.

Celebrating Our Understanding

In the first section of this part, you explored a five-stage review process to analyze and resolve an ethical dilemma. In the next section of this part, you used a scenario to practice the five-stage review process for resolving ethical dilemmas. You learned that ethical dilemmas are complex in nature and do not have easy solutions. You also learned that the review process takes you on a journey that strategically moves you stage by stage toward the analysis and resolution of ethical dilemmas. An important part of that journey is understanding the need for professional judgment and professional change. You now have a process to guide you as you encounter challenging ethical situations with children, families, colleagues, and community.

Celebrate your learning in Part III! You have now expanded your understanding of how the NAEYC Code can be used to resolve ethical dilemmas.

:

Resources and References

Brophy-Herb, H. E., Kostelnik, M. J., & Stein, L. C. (2001). A developmental approach to teaching about ethics using the NAEYC Code of Ethical Conduct. *Young Children, 1,* 80–84.

Feeney, S., & Freeman, N. (1999). *Ethics and the early childhood educator: Using the NAEYC Code.* Washington, DC: NAEYC.

Feeney, S., & K. Kipnis. 1998. *Code of ethical conduct and statement of commitment* (Rev. ed.). Washington, DC: NAEYC

Nash, R. (1996). *"Real world" ethics: Frameworks for educators and human service professionals.* New York: Teachers College Press.

National Research Council and Institute of Medicine (2000). *From neurons to neighborhoods. The science of early childhood development.* Committee on Integrating the Science of Early Childhood Development. Jack P. Shonkoff & Deborah A. Phillips, (Eds.). Board on Children, Youth, and Families, Commission on Behavioral and Social Sciences and Education. Washington, DC: National Academy Press.

Reynolds, M. (1996). *Guiding young children: A child-centered approach* (2nd ed.). Mountain View, CA: Mayfield Publishing.

Spencer, L. (1989). *Winning through participation.* Dubuque, IA: Kendall Hunt.

Part IV

EXTENDING OUR UNDERSTANDING OF ETHICS IN EARLY CARE AND EDUCATION

Issues in Ethics in Early Care and Education

Thinking in Different Ways About Ethics in Care and Education

EXTENDING OUR UNDERSTANDING OF ETHICS IN EARLY CARE AND EDUCATION

In the previous parts of this book, you have had an opportunity to learn about the historical development, framework, content, and context of the NAEYC Code of Ethical Conduct. The previous parts have assisted you in moving from an awareness level to a deeper understanding of the NAEYC Code of Ethical Conduct. This understanding enabled you to practice using the five-stage review process for resolving ethical dilemmas. In Part IV you will explore two key issues in ethics in early care and education and be given opportunities to think about ethics in different ways. Extending your understanding of ethics in early care and education is an important disposition for early care and education ethical practice. This extension of understanding will enable you to think about ethics now and in the future.

GUIDING QUESTION

❏ How do we extend our understanding of ethics in early care and education?

To assist the reader in answering the guiding question for Part IV, we will examine two key issues related to ethics in early care and education. Those issues include ethical identity and ethics education.

Issues in Ethics in Early Care and Education

What I Know Activity

List below what you consider to be issues in ethics in early care and education.

-
-
-

As mentioned before, ethics in early care and education represents complex and oftentimes ambiguous ways of thinking. In this section, we will have a discussion about two of the many complexities and ambiguities that we will call issues, a concept we have chosen to use to extend our understanding of the ethics in early care and education. For this section of Part IV, we have selected two issues to think about. One is ethical identity and the other is ethics education. We selected these issues because of their currency and importance and impact on ethical practice in the field. To begin our discussion, we will focus on the issue of ethical identity in early care and education.

When we think of ethical identity, we think first of moving "from beings members of the general public to becoming fully practicing early childhood professionals" (Hayden, 2000, p. 34). For example, you are a citizen of your state. However, when you decide upon a career in early care and education, you become a member of a profession. This membership entails an understanding and an adherence to the shared value of the profession. Another way of seeing this may be through the use of the term "professionalism". Professionalism includes ethical practice. To engage in ethical practice, we must have an ethical identity, which is defined by Newman and Pollnitz (2001) as: "a sense of the professional self that includes the confidence and the competence to make sound and sensitive ethical judgments" (p. 40). What is important to know is that ethical identity is the part of our professional self that allows us to do our daily work. For example, our professional self includes knowledge and skills in child development and agreement with the professions value. We can say that when an issue arises related to the appropriateness of an activity, we use this aspect of our professional self, i.e., knowledge of child development and values of the profession, to make the appropriate decision or judgment regarding the situation. Using this logic, we can continue to say that our professional self is inclusive of an ethical identity. We construct our ethical identity from our knowledge, skills, dispositions, and value from ethics education and experience and our ability to dialogue and reflect about ethical dilemmas both individually and with others. The process of constructing ethical identity occurs over time. It is important to understand that constructing an ethical identity is a developmental process and cannot be hurried but can be supported through ethics education. Now that we know <u>how</u> we construct our ethical identity, we need to think about <u>why</u> it is important to construct our ethical identity.

Ethical identity is a key factor in ethical practice and resolving ethical dilemmas. Practitioners who have not developed ethical identity may violate professional value, such as the one that states: "Appreciating childhood as a unique and valuable stage of the human life cycle" (NAEYC Code). A teacher might use an inappropriate guidance technique based on his/her lack of appreciation for the uniqueness of childhood. In contrast, a teacher who has developed an ethical identity might use an appropriate guidance technique because he or she does understand the uniqueness of the child's particular stage of development. We can conclude that the teacher's behavior emerged from his or her ethical identity. It is important, then, to construct an ethical identity to prevent harm to children and families.

Next, we need to think about the opportunities available to developing professionals to construct their ethical identity. Newman and Pollnitz (2001) suggest that early childhood teacher educators "need to be proactive about modifying courses to better facilitate students development of sound ethical identities by helping them develop ethically sound responses to problematic situations" (p. 40). What it seems that Newman and Pollnitz are suggesting is that early care and education faculty in institutions of higher education must provide opportunities for students to gain knowledge of ethics and practice developing skills in responding to complex situations. For many faculty it is not as easy as it sounds. We will now examine our second issue, that of ethics education.

As university professors working in early care and education Associate and Bachelors degree programs, we believe that ethics education at the undergraduate level highly impacts ethical practice in the field. . Although research does not yet suggest that ethics education makes ethical practitioners, it is the opinion of the authors and others (Newman & Pollnitz, 2001) that ethics education contributes to ethical practice. Thus, we sought resources to assist us in our teaching about the NAEYC Code of Ethical Conduct and issues in ethics in early care and education. During our search, we realized that other than *Ethics and the Early Childhood Educator: Using the NAEYC Code* (Feeney and Freeman, 1999), there were no specific texts that addressed the use of the NAEYC Code. We found either mere mention of the code or 3–4 page descriptions of the code in several early childhood textbooks, but did not believe those resources were sufficient to provide students with a foundation in ethics. In 2000, NAEYC published *Teaching the NAEYC Code of Ethical Conduct* (Feeney, Freeman, & Moravcik, 2000), a text that added to the teaching resources of early care and education faculty in institutions of higher education. Our process of searching for resources led us to believe that additional texts would assist faculty in their responsibilities of ethics education. For that reason, the authors created this text to add another choice for early childhood teacher educators. However, the issue extends beyond resources to accessibility of ethics education.

Ethics education is important for practitioners because it gives students/practitioners the necessary knowledge and skills to make ethical judgments based on the shared value of the profession. Ethical judgments made in isolation may not support the shared value of the profession and may conflict with the professions stated ethical responsibilities. The conflicts that occur in relationship to ethics issues include but are not limited to personal, legal, employment, and social theory problems (Newman, Coombe, Arefi, Davidson & Humphries (1999). These conflicts may, in fact, bring harm to children and/or families and/or to the practitioner. Pre-service students and practitioners need opportunities to practice and develop skills to avoid potential conflicts.

Because ethics education resources are available does not mean that practitioners have access to ethics education. Thus, access to ethics education becomes a major issue for the field. One would like to assume that all pre-service students receive ethics education in one or more courses in their teacher preparation program. However, in looking through course catalogues at the Associate and Bachelors degree levels, it is not apparent that there are either specific courses that focus on ethics education or substantial sections of courses that focus on ethics education. Therefore, we cannot categorically say that all teacher candidates have had sufficient ethics education preparation. What is left for practitioners, then, is to seek ethics education through conferences, pre and in-service workshops, individual reading, collegial relationships and other avenues. We have found that ethics education is offered sporadically at national conferences, e.g., NAEYC and Early Childhood Reconceptualizing conferences. What is glaring is that ethics education is almost non-existent in many state and local conferences and very often not addressed in individual program staff development activities or meetings. It seems that there are large gaps in the quantity of ethics education opportunities as well as gaps in accessibility to the existing ethics education opportunities.

Knowing the current landscape of ethics education, we need to envision an ethics education system that is accessible to all early care and education pre-service students and practitioners. A point of departure for accessibility of ethics education might be Parker Palmers (1998) suggestion that we create a *movement* in ethics education. What that would entail is that each one of us in collaboration with our colleagues advocate at all levels for ethics education. What a *movement* means is that multiple shared voices would generate energy to create those intentional spaces to provide ethics education, all members of the early care and education profession., e.g., specific college courses, conference tracks in ethics, and institutionalization of ethics training in early care and education work sites. This might mean an introduction for some members or it might mean an extension of the dialogue about ethics in early care and education for other members. The key outcome of this endeavor will be that ethics education will become one of the priorities of the profession. We believe that students have a very important role in this advocacy effort.

There are many ways to advocate for ethics education. We have chosen to share Parker Palmers stages to create a movement. Our main focus at this moment is to share a strategy for advocating for ethics education rather than creating a specific ethics education system. We believe that through the process of creating a *movement*, the ethics education system will emerge. Parker Palmer (1998) suggests the following stages:

"Stage 1. Isolated individuals make an inward decision to live *"divided no more,"* finding a center for their lives outside of institutions.

Stage 2. These individuals begin to discover one another and form *communities of congruence* that offer mutual support and opportunities to develop a shared vision.

Stage 3. These communities start *going public,* learning to convert their private concerns into the public issues they are and receiving vital critiques in the process.

Stage 4. A system of *alternative rewards* emerges to sustain the movement's vision and to put pressure for change on the standard institutional reward system" (p. 166).

Now that we have learned about Parker Palmers stages to create a movement, we will suggest specific advocacy strategies that you can take to advocate for ethics education. Let's begin by looking at Stage 1. Stage 1 basically tells us that early care and education personnel need to rethink their professional service from that of isolation to the context of a group, the profession rather than as isolated individuals working with children and families. Once we work through our isolation and begin to seek out others, we are moving into Stage 2. By rethinking ourselves as part of a group, we can then move ourselves and our struggle, in our case, ethics education, to a group focus. The benefit of this stage is that individuals do not have to wrestle with hard issues by themselves but can reach out to others to assist them. Stage 3 suggests going beyond our small groups to present our issue to a larger community who then provides feedback about the issue. Movement occurs when we go beyond our small group to the larger community. The larger community can then assist in sustaining the shared vision by creating checks and balances for the stakeholders. What that means is that the group maintains strong value about ethics education, but also listens to the larger group. It is the larger group that assists in systems change. When we move from Stage 3 to Stage 4, we see changes in systems. Changes in systems often bring rewards to its participants that they didn't have prior to the change. In this case, the rewards would be an ethics education system advocated for by the membership, not just the leaders of NAEYC.

At this time, the authors see themselves in Stage 3 of the *movement*. Thus far, we individually perceived a need for ethics education. From this awareness, we began holding conversations with each other and others (colleagues, students) regarding ethics education. We moved into the public by discussing issues in ethics education in national conferences and through this book. Our goal is to encourage further public dialogue on ethics education resulting in a formalized system of ethics   education.

We have explored two key issues related to ethics in early care and education; ethical identity and ethics education. For early care and education practitioners to develop their own ethical identity, they need ethics education at the early and continuing stages of their professional development. Currently, there is a gap in ethics education in our profession. This gap is problematic to us, because it has implications for ethical practice. Pre-service and in-service practitioners need accessible ethics education to support their ethical practice. As we all work toward an ethics education advocacy movement, we will have additional opportunities to learn, dialogue, and think about ethics in different ways.

What follows is an opportunity for you to synthesize your learning by responding to reflective questions.

What I Have Learned

Reflective Questions

Reflective Questions

If you are in a classroom setting, "Think, Pair, and Share" (Wolfe, 2000). Think about your response to the questions, find a partner, and share your responses. If you are not in a classroom setting, share your thoughts with a friend.

1. What have I learned about how to become an ethics advocate?
2. What are my feelings about ethics education?
3. Why do I think ethics education is important?
4. How will I advocate for ethics education?

Thinking in Different Ways About Ethics in Early Care and Education

**What I Know Activity**

Mindsets

A part of our understanding in ethics in early care and education is for practitioners to think about ethics in different ways. Newman and Pollnitz (2001) tell us that "issues relating to ethical judgement are multidimensional and are influenced significantly by the rapidly changing socio-economic and political climate in which we live and work" (p. 40). Knowing ethical judgment is affected by a changing society; we have no choice but to view ethics as a dynamic process requiring practitioners to think about ethics in different ways. In this section, we will review the developmental process of ethics in the United States as well as review a perspective suggested by our Australian colleagues, Newman and Pollnitz. Following our discussion of varying perspectives on ethics in early care and education, the authors will use ethics research to engage the readers in extending their thinking about ethics in early care and education.

Ethics in early childhood education has been in a developmental process since the 1970s. In an earlier chapter you read about the historical development of the NAEYC Code and learned that much discussion preceded the development of the NAEYC Code. During that time the profession determined that it was important to address the issue of professional ethics. According to Newman (2000), the discussion of ethics by the profession constituted the "first age of ethics" (p. 42). As the profession acted on these discussions, developed a code of ethical conduct for the membership of the profession, and continued the dialogue about ethics in the profession, according to Newman (2000), ethics entered into "the second age" (p. 42). During this "second age", NAEYC leaders disseminated the approved NAEYC Code through publications and conferences and developed additional resource materials. The membership enhanced its awareness of ethics, the importance of ethics in the profession, and the need to use the NAEYC Code. As the ethics agenda gained momentum, the process moved into "the third age" (Newman, 2000, p. 43). Newman (2000) describes "the third age" as "a time of reconceptualising the use of our codes and guidelines" (p. 43) because of the challenges inherent in a changing society.

As we look at business practices in the United States during the last decade, we have seen that ethics issues have come to the forefront of corporate America, higher education, and other public and private sector institutions. The emergence of so many situations that have drawn our attention to ethics suggests that we need to revisit ethics and look at ethics in different ways. During "the third age", the responsibility of professional leaders is to invite the continuing discussion of the relevance of current documents and thinking in relationship to the ethics of the profession. As our society changes and the context in which professional work changes, ethics as we know them may need rethinking and revision. Reconceptualizing offers practitioners opportunities to reflect on their current practice and the guidance that supports their practice. Kennedy (2001) tells us, "Codes of ethics are about the value which the group who devise the code believe are important to that group's identity and survival" (p. 17). An important lesson to learn from this statement is that codes of ethical conduct were developed at a particular moment in history. As times change, the code that was developed at that moment of history may no longer reflect the value that support the "identity and survival" of the group. It then becomes necessary to think about ethics in ways that are different from the way ethics was thought about before.

In the last few pages, we have focused on the idea of a changing society as a means to think differently about ethics in early care and education. To continue the conversation, we will now focus on a review of an aspect of ethics, that is, codification. Codification refers to the placement into a document of agreed- upon value of a profession and serves as a behavioral guide for ethical practice. NAEYC has selected codification as its documentation of ethics in early care and education. Codification has served the purpose of heightening awareness of ethics to the NAEYC membership. The codification process has pointed out that the profession needs more research in the area of ethics. The codification process has also contributed to new forums to discuss ethics in early care and education. What we need to know is that codes are controversial. For example, Kennedy (2001) asks: "If codes of ethics cannot guarantee ethical practice, then why would a profession want to adopt one?" (p. 20).

Codes also become controversial because they are perceived as the ultimate truths about the professions shared value, when, in fact, what is missing is the knowledge that codes are a representation of value for a particular time in history. For example, the NAEYC Code was developed in the early 1970s. At that time we, as a society, were beginning to emerge as a technological society. Thirty years later, we can now say that we are a technological society. The question now is, "Have our value changed as a result of becoming a technological society and how has this change affected our value as represented in the NAEYC Code?" In earlier times we believed in the professional autonomy of practitioners. Early care and education teachers could close their door and provide what they believed were appropriate environments, curriculum, and learning activities, typically without continuous oversight by administrators or parents. Now we can find television monitors in early care and education classrooms that are placed primarily for protection of children and practitioners but which, in fact, intrude upon professional autonomy because directors have continuous viewing of a teacher's classroom.

Controversies that stem from value changes show themselves when group's value are questionable because the principles upon which they are based are out of context, when codes are the only avenue for representing ethics, or when groups do not have enforcement policies for the code. Although all professions have adopted codes of ethics, we cannot say that all practitioners demonstrate ethical practice (Newman, 2000) or that all professions have enforcement policies for their codes. For example, an early care and education professional who violates a major principle of the code such as P-1.1 and does do harm to a child will receive no sanctions from the professional organization, although the practitioner may be terminated from his/her employment.

Another idea to consider about codification is that currently NAEYC has used the code as the only way to think about ethics and the dilemmas associated with it. One of our colleagues in Australia (Kennedy, 2001) suggests "if the code of ethics is to remain a key resource for professional development in Australia, I would contend that the profession ought to continue to examine and debate the nature of value intended in that document in the first step of determining its continued relevance for the field" (p. 24). As you learned earlier, the NAEYC Code of Ethical Conduct is scheduled for revision. This revision should include opportunities for the membership to dialogue about the underlying value of the NAEYC Code. Woodrow (2001) states, "There is a risk that codes might be seen as endpoints in themselves and their existence might limit or constrain the search for alternative ways of understanding and treating ethics" (p. 28). We would suggest that during the revision process the following questions be addressed: 1) How is the profession addressing the issue of inclusivity of diverse early care and education personnel? 2) Given the current context of our society and knowing that change is a continuous process, what are the issues relevant to ethical practice? 3) Given the current and changing context of our society, what are the values that need to be re-examined? and 4) What are frameworks other than codification that might address the issues in early care and education? Responses to these questions will move the profession to think about ethics in different ways.

To think about ethics in different ways, we suggest we continue to ask questions about ethics in our profession. Many of our members in this country and others are asking those questions through action research. Action research as we envision it is a means for practitioners to gather information about the use of ethics in their daily work. What is distinct about the action research is that as practitioners gather this information they realize that it is not the information itself that gives them the answers to their questions. What helps action researchers in their work is the understanding that the information gathered is always in a context of "power, knowledge, and truth meaning (MacNaughton, Smith, 2001, p. 33). For example, different groups have different truths. As an action researcher, if we were researching applied ethics in the context of a group of thieves, the information I would gather is that "Thieves may value confidentiality (a common principle within codes of ethics) which prohibits revealing information about a fellow thief to the police "(Kennedy, 2001, p. 19). What is glaring from this example is that if the action researcher were to view the information out of the context of the group of thieves, the action researcher might conclude that ethical behavior for thieves is not to tell on each other. However, looking at this situation in another context, that is, "power, knowledge, and truth meaning," the information the action researcher gathered takes on a different meaning. Action research, then, can be that avenue through which the profession can learn more about the use of ethics and document that learning. This learning can scaffold us to think about ethics in different ways. How we see this happening in the field will be our next conversation.

Action research affords the profession the opportunity to create new ways for bringing many voices into the discussion about ethics. We believe that if higher education institutions in partnership with community programs were to launch action research programs, valuable information would emerge to support our knowledge base in ethics. What we propose is to convene a national forum of action researchers to begin thinking about ethics in different ways. The result of the national forum would expand knowledge and resources regarding ethics and support the professions continuing engagement in ethics (Woodrow, 2001).

Another way besides action research that we can think about ethics differently is in the context of caring. We have a history in the early care and education profession of using the context of caring for the work we do. Cherrington (2001) suggests that in early care and education we also consider the thinking of Carol Gilligan (1982) and Nel Noddings (1984). Both of these women support the notion that central to our thinking in ethics should be the concept of caring for others. They believe it is this concept that should guide ethical practice. What is inherent in this concept is that there is a mutual responsibility for care. By thinking about ethics in the context of caring, practitioners can then see ethics in a different way.

Thinking about ethics in different ways requires practitioners to question their value, beliefs, and ideas about ethics and its application. Thinking about ethics requires practitioners to engage in and reflect upon caring, courage, and creative thinking as was mentioned in Part III. It is this reflection that will move practitioners into the action of thinking about ethics in different ways.

What I Have Learned

Reflective Questions

If you are in a classroom setting, "Think, Pair, and Share" (Wolfe, 2000). Think about your response to the questions, find a partner, and share your responses. If you are not in a classroom setting, share your thoughts with a friend.

1. What do you remember about the discussions of thinking about ethics in different ways in early care and education?
2. What are your feelings about being encouraged to think about ethics in different ways?
3. Why is it important to think about ethics in different ways?
4. What would you tell your colleagues about thinking about ethics in different ways?

Celebrating Our Understanding

What we have learned in Part IV is that there are a variety of issues in ethics in early care and education. We explored two of those issues, ethical identity and ethics education. We also learned about thinking differently about ethics in early care and education because of the changing context and value in our society. What is exciting to know is that you now have extended your understanding of ethics in early care and education. This extension of your understanding is important because it gives you new information for your ethical thinking and practice. As you ethically think and practice, we challenge you to actively participate in future revisions of the NAEYC Code.

Celebrate your effort in completing Part IV and continue your construction of early care and education ethics.

Resources and References

Cherrington, S. (2001). *Australian Journal of Early Childhood, 26,* 14–18.

Feeney, S., & Freeman, N. (1999). *Ethics and the early childhood educator: Using the NAEYC Code.* Washington, DC: NAEYC.

Feeney, S., Freeman, N., & Moravcik, E. (2000). *Teaching the NAEYC Code of Ethical Conduct.* Washington, DC: NAEYC

Feeney, S., & K. Kipnis. 1998. *Code of ethical conduct and statement of commitment* (Rev. ed.). Washington, DC: NAEYC

Hayden, J. (Ed.). (2000). *Landscapes in early childhood education.* New York: Peter Lang.

Kennedy, A. (2001). The nature of value in early childhood education: An analysis of the AECA code of ethics. *Australian Journal of Early Childhood, 25,* 43.

MacNaughton, G., & Smith, K. (2001). Helping students make tough decisions wisely: The challenge of ethical inquiry. *Australian Journal of Early Childhood, 26,* 39–42, 44 & 47.

Newman, L. (2000). Ethical leadership or leadership in ethics? *Australian*

Journal of Early Childhood, 25, 43.

Newman, L, Coombe, K, Arefi, M., Davidson, F., & Humphries, J. (1999). Facing hard questions: Ethics for early childhood fieldwork programs. *Australian Journal of Early Childhood, 25,* 43.

Newman, L., & Pollnitz, L. (2001). Helping students make tough decisions wisely. The challenge of ethical inquiry. *Australian Journal of Early Childhood, 26,* 39–42, 44 & 47

Palmer, P. (1998). The courage to teach. Exploring the inner landscape of a teacher's life. San Francisco, CA: Jossey-Bass Publishers.

Woodrow, C. (2001). Ethics in early childhood: continuing the conversations. *Australian Journal of Early Childhood, 26*(4), 6 (6)